pencil
mach

PAST AND FUTURE IN ANCIENT HISTORY

Publications of the Association of Ancient Historians I

Chester G. Starr

University of Michigan

UNIVERSITY
PRESS OF
AMERICA

LANHAM • NEW YORK • LONDON

British Cataloging in Publication Information Available

Library of Congress Cataloging-in-Publication Data

Starr, Chester G., 1914-
   Past and future in ancient history.

   (Publications of the Association of Ancient
Historians ; 1)
   Bibliography: p.
   1. Greece—History—To 146 B.C.—Historiography.
2. Rome—Historiography. I. Title. II. Series.
DE8.S69   1987   938   87-6296
ISBN 0-8191-6301-5
ISBN 0-8191-6302-3 (pbk.)

Co-published by arrangement with the
Association of Ancient Historians

To all my students
who incited me to remain
intellectually alive

ACKNOWLEDGMENTS

At their annual meeting in 1985, the members of the Association of Ancient Historians approved the commencement of a series of occasional publications supporting a principal aim of the Association — to further the teaching of, and research in Ancient History in Canada and the U.S.A. Chester G. Starr, who served as the Association's first president, was commissioned to write the premiere volume — an overview of contemporary historical scholarship in Greek and Roman studies. Subsequent volumes will attempt to inform teachers, scholars and students about current trends in the study of the ancient Near East and the worlds of Greece and Rome.

John W. Eadie of Michigan State University and Stanley M. Burstein of California State University, Los Angeles, joined me to form a publication committee which supervised the production of the first volume. My colleague at the Pennsylvania State University, Paul B. Harvey, Jr., assisted in seeing the manuscript through the technical preparation of camera-ready copy. We are grateful that the editorial board of University Press of America agreed to co-publish the series.

Eugene N. Borza, President
Association of Ancient Historians

CONTENTS

PREFACE

Let me invite thoughtful attention to the two purposes of this monograph as a general survey of recent trends and possible future areas of investigation in all fields of ancient history. In assessing major contributions to our views I have cited works which most of us would consider fundamental, such as those of Brown, Dodds, Marrou, Syme, and others; especially for books before World War II I have not felt it always necessary to give publishing data. Elsewhere I have noted articles and books which specifically illustrate points in my text. This is not a bibliographical essay; if I have omitted any study which its author considers should have been included I can only apologize. As far as possible preference has been given to books and journals in English or translated.

In the second aspect I feel diffident about identifying future areas of research. Who can tell when a bright student will revolutionize our concepts or methods of approach in any area? My comments in this respect must be taken as personal evaluations and certainly are not presented as a quarry for dissertation subjects.

Finally I have seen no reason why the following pages should always be dull though they must be sober. My lighter comments, however, are not intended to ridicule any colleague. *Tolle et lege* — the only Latin or Greek you will find in this work apart from titles of officials.

Ann Arbor   Chester G. Starr
December 28, 1985

I

GREECE

The most majestic history of Greece to the present day was written by the Victorian banker, George Grote, a work still to be admired even though he could not make use of the archeological discoveries from Schliemann onward. In an inaugural lecture at the University of London Momigliano praised Grote for his "combination of passionate moral and political interests, vast learning, and respect for the evidence."[1]

Yet Momigliano went on to observe that "to-day it is Greek History that presents most difficulties both to the teacher and to the researcher . . . all students of Ancient History know in their heart that Greek history is passing through a crisis." To support his pessimism he briefly suggested the lack of an adequate statistical base for the investigation of social and economic aspects, unilateral approaches by Marxists and others, and the separation of political and cultural frameworks. More critical in my judgment is another point he raises, to wit, that many students these days disregard Grote's warnings on the need to apply proper historical standards to the criticism of our evidence, limited as it is. I shall return shortly to this serious problem.

Going beyond Momigliano, we may note that more general ideological and methodological disagreements also cause uncertainty, confusion, and difficulty. Some of these will concern us later, but let me point out a few here: Do we judge slaves or aristocrats more important? What then do we make of the elitist character of Greek civilization? Are we "liberals" these days? Do we favor democracy or egalitarianism? Can we still idealize ancient Athens, as the Victorians did?[2] And finally is it more important or "useful" to study political history or cultural evolution – or is there a distinction to be made?

Enough for the moment of questions which can be endlessly debated; in any case, as Murray has observed, "We mostly operate with a few firmly held ideas and a strong belief in the virtues of empiricism" – a procedure not just of Greek historians but of at least

[1]G. Grote, *History of Greece*, 12 vols. (London, 1846-56); A. Momigliano, *George Grote and the Study of Greek History* (London, 1952),

[2]R. Jenkyns, *The Victorians and Ancient Greece* (Oxford, 1980); F.M. Turner, *The Greek Heritage in Victorian Britain* (New Haven, 1981).

GREECE

English-speaking students of any era in the past.[3] Whatever Momigliano's doubts the fact is that the exploration of Greek history has in recent decades broadened out chronologically to encompass the formative centuries before 500 B.C. and at the other end to more careful study of the fourth century; geographically we now raise our gaze from just Athens and Sparta; and finally far more aspects of Greek development are receiving their proper attention.

Here I shall omit the Minoan and Mycenaean ages as still lying primarily in the hands of archeologists, though the light thrown by Linear B tablets on palace economies and public administration can never be disregarded as a foil to historic Greece. The centuries after the fall of Mycenae down to 500 – the Dark Ages and the age of expansion (or lyric/archaic era) – now can be seen much more clearly as the decisive period in which the political, religious, and cultural framework of classic times was being established.

This great advance rests upon three major foundations. First, Homeric scholarship has attained a general consensus on the manner of consolidation of the epics in their final form and usually dates the end of the process to some point in the eighth century. The characteristics of the society depicted in the *Iliad* and *Odyssey* have also been more properly assessed.[4] Secondly, a number of basic monographs have explored the development of armor, figurines, pins, alphabet, and above all pottery styles.[5] In this last area the steady elaboration of the Protogeometric style can be followed through the German excavations in the cemetery of the Kerameikos, the single most important archeological exploration since the days of Schliemann and Evans, but similar development is visible at Argos and elsewhere.[6] Thirdly, archeological work all over Greece has markedly increased our information, and often has upset conventional views; thus, for example, no major building was known from the Dark Ages

[3]O. Murray, *Journal of Hellenic Studies*, 103 (1983), p. 198.

[4]M.I. Finley, *The World of Odysseus*, (rev. ed.; New York, 1978), challenged by A.M. Snodgrass, *Journal of Hellenic Studies*, 94 (1974), pp. 114-25; J. Bouzek, *Homer and the Heroic Age* (London, 1973); and on warfare the ingenious study by P.A.L. Greenhalgh, *Early Greek Warfare* (Cambridge, 1973).

[5]On the alphabet see L.H. Jeffery, *The Local Scripts of Archaic Greece* (Oxford, 1961), which thows more light on the diversity already visible in archaic Greece than does her dreary survey, geographically arranged, *Archaic Greece: The City-State c. 700-500 B.C.* (London, 1976).

[6]Beyond the extensive reports in *Kerameikos* see the engaging essay by G. Karo, *An Attic Cemetary* (Philadelphia, 1943).

until the English uncovered a heroon of the tenth century at Lefkandi.[7] Renfrew and others have engaged in intensive field work on Melos, as also Jameson in the Argolid and McDonald's team in Messenia. Hammond in particular has shown in various essays the necessity of detailed geographical knowledge of a battle site.[8] No study of Greek history written more than two decades ago is now adequate for the period before 500, and the current works devoted to this era will themselves be outdated in the future.[9]

Since I have concentrated on the formative stage of Greek civilization and political structure in several works I could happily extend my remarks here at length, but let me emphasize that these pages are not intended to offer a reconstruction of Greek history. What then are some of the major areas of debate in respect to early Greece? Eventually Hellenic culture was sharply stamped by aristocratic attitudes; how far back can we trace aristocracies and how influential were the upper classes in the creation of the *polis*?[10] Can we find the basic lineaments of the Hellenic outlook in the Dark Ages, as I have argued in several studies; or does it appear only in the more fully illuminated seventh century, as others insist? A very important development, affecting all later Greek history, was the colonization of western and northern shores. As far as dates are concerned the clarification of the stages of Corinthian vases by Payne and Benson has produced a solid yardstick,[11] but there is still vigorous debate over the question whether the Phoenicians preceded the Greeks in western waters; if one accepts legendary dates, they did so, but we have no physical evidence at Phoenician sites until the beginning of

---

[7]See provisionally *Archaeological Reports for 1981-2*, pp. 16-17; *for 1982-83*, p.13.

[8]C. Renfrew and M. Wagstaff, ed., *An Island Polity* (Cambridge, 1982); J. Wiseman, *The Land of the Ancient Corinthians* (Göteborg, 1978); N.G.L. Hammond, *Studies in Greek History* (Oxford, 1973) and his surveys of Epirus (Oxford, 1967) and more recently Macedonia, 2 vols. to date (Oxford, 1972-79).

[9]In addition to works listed in previous notes there is a wide variety of recent studies in English by Coldstream, Desborough, Finley, Murray, Snodgrass, and Starr; in *Individual and Community: The Rise of the Polis 800-500 B.C.* (New York, 1986), I give a detailed bibliography.

[10]A.W.H. Adkins, *Moral Values and Political Behaviour in Ancient Greece* (London, 1972), is certain that aristocracy goes back to Homeric times; Snodgrass and Starr are doubtful. W. Donlan, *The Aristocratic Ideal in Archaic Greece* (Lawrence, Kans., 1980), is useful.

[11]H. Payne, *Necrocorinthia* (Oxford, 1931); J.L. Benson, *Die Geschichte der korinthischen Vasen* (Basel, 1953). Payne was a genius whose every work was a masterpiece; he died much too early. See the memoir, *An Affair of the Heart* (Penguin, 1961), by his wife Dilys Powell.

the eighth century.[12] Long ago Gwynn established the orthodox view that the aim of the Greeks was to settle surplus population on agricultural lands; this was challenged to some extent by Blakeway in the 1930's but has more recently come under heavy attack. The first settlement of the Greeks in the west was on the rocky island of Ischia (Pithecusae) and clearly was intended to tap the metal resources of Etruria; at many sites in southern Italy and Sicily, both on the coast and in the interior, Greek pottery appears before there were settlers in that area.[13] But can we speak of "trade" in this connection? Some scholars insist that exchanges of physical objects must be explained in terms of gift exchange, following the well-known theory of Mauss in *Le Don*; others feel that if the Athenian potter Nicosthenes deliberately molded vases in Etruscan shapes and used for decoration myths favored by the Etruscans true trading patterns had been established at least by the sixth century.[14]

Another area where significant changes have occurred is in the exploration of the rise of tyrannies. In the 1920's Ure (known as "Peahen" from his initials) argued that the appearance of coinage upset earlier political patterns; tyrants were the vehicle by which the emergent commercial and industrial sectors gained a voice.[15] Occasionally purely factual evidence is decisive in supporting or demolishing theories; we now are certain that silver coinage began in the Aegean only after tyrannies had emerged, and in any case Ure dated commercial and industrial activity too early — not that these "bourgeois" elements ever gained power in any Greek state. More recently Andrewes, following a view expressed by Aristotle about hoplites, has sought to prove that consolidation of the hoplite classes, which manned the phalanxes from the early seventh century on, was the causative factor, but here too one must be doubtful; how did this purported class gain sufficient cohesion and independence of stance

---

[12]A recent symposium on this topic is edited by H.G. Niemeyer, *Phönizier im Westen* (Mainz, 1982).

[13]A. Gwynn, *Journal of Hellenic Studies*, 38 (1918), pp. 88-123; for Blakeway, *Annual of the British School of Athens*, 33 (1932-3), pp. 170-208. See recently A.J. Graham, *Colony and Mother City in Ancient Greece* (Manchester, 1974), and his chapters in *Cambridge Ancient History*, 3, part 3 (though his views on Pithecusae are properly queried by the editors); J. Boardman, *The Greeks Overseas* (rev. ed.; London, 1980).

[14]M.M. Eisman, *Archaeology*, 28 (1975), pp. 76-83, and other studies.

[15]P.N. Ure, *The Origin of Tyranny* (Cambridge, 1922).

in the early *polis*?[16] Probably the most useful comment on the appearance of tyrants is an essay by Drews, which emphasizes their use of mercenaries to gain mastery for their own selfish ends.[17]

The political figures in archaic times who continue to elicit debate are Solon and Cleisthenes; both their objectives and their actual reforms have been explored in a continuous stream of articles which need not be discussed at length here. It may be noted, however, that Athens, which we take as a paradigm of Greek political development, actually was unique in its early unification, in its willingness to choose Solon as archon and reconciler at a time of violent upheaval, and finally in the dexterity with which Cleisthenes set its patterns of government for the following two centuries and more.

To conclude an all-too-brief survey of early Greece there is marked disagreement as to the extent to which we may trust legend and other much later "evidence" in our reconstructions. In his preface Grote laid down the principle that "the law respecting sufficiency of evidence ought to be the same for ancient times as for modern", so he began only in 776 and even then found trustworthy information to be thin; he described the legends without pronouncing on their historicity. Alas, many students are now pre-Grotean in their willingness to manipulate very dubious materials; the result may be intellectually magnificent, but it remains a gossamer, "a pleasing romance in place of half-known and perplexing realities," to quote Grote once more. One ingenious weaver of webs thus presents us with a Spartan reformer in Crete in the eighth century solely on the base of a comment in Pausanias nearly a millennium later; this will not do.[18] Down almost to 500 we should rely primarily on the physical evidence, continuously augmented by the archeologists, and can admit literary sources only if they are really contemporary; Herodotus himself ventured to go back no more than three generations in recounting the tales he had heard from many sources and did not always trust even these.

---

[16]A. Andrewes, *The Greek Tyrants* (London, 1956); on hoplites see also A.M. Snodgrass, "The Hoplite Reform and History," *Journal of Hellenic Studies*, 85 (1965), pp. 110-22.

[17]R. Drews, *Historia*, 21 (1972), pp. 129-49, now also in K.H. Kinzl, ed. *Die ältere Tyrannis bis zu den Perserkriegen* (Darmstadt, 1979); H.W. Pleket, *Talanta*, 1 (1969), pp. 19-61.

[18]G.L. Huxley, *Early Sparta* (Cambridge, Mass., 1962), p. 27; on the question of method see my essay, *Rivista di filologia*, 92 (1964), p. 5-23, now in my *Essays on Ancient History* (Leiden, 1979), pp. 103-21.

GREECE

The fifth century is one of the most creative eras in all Western history, and continues to draw the attention of most Greek historians. One new source for the period is the Themistocles decree, a resolution ordering the evacuation of Attica before the Persian invasion of 480, but since its discovery debate has swirled about its authenticity.[19] Equally vigorous contention also arises with regard to the dating of Athenian decrees; perhaps nowhere else does so much turn on one simple physical change such as the shift of Athenian stone cutters from carving a sigma with three notches to one with four strokes.[20] The extent to which we can use Athenian tragedies to illuminate more than intellectual and religious attitudes also remains contentious, though greater caution in this regard seems more evident of late.[21]

It is probably time to declare a moratorium on studies of the peculiar ways of the Spartans, especially those which use the decline of Laconian pottery to prove the evils of militarism. I do not speak altogether in jest; Laconian exports fell at the same time and for the same reason as the virtual disappearance of Corinthian vases from overseas markets, yet Spartan metalworkers continued to turn out masterpieces such as the crater of Vix and other bronzes found at Olympia down through the fifth century. The political role of Sparta in the Greek state system is also almost always underestimated; it was a vital balance wheel which provided leaders by land and sea whom the allies could accept in the defense against Xerxes and later it was the state which was to liberate the Aegean from Athenian "enslave-

---

[19]M.H. Jameson, *Hesperia*, 29 (1960), pp. 198-223. The most complete attack is by C. Habicht, *Hermes*, 89 (1961), pp. 1-35, with whom I agree. Contra, C.W. Fornara, *American Historical Review*, 73 (1967), pp. 425-33.

[20]The debate was begun by H.G. Mattingly, *Historia*, 10 (1961), pp. 148-88, immediately rebutted by B.D. Meritt and H.T. Wade-Gery, *Journal of Hellenic Studies*, 82 (1962), pp. 67ff., and R. Meiggs, *Harvard Studies in Classical Philology*, 67 (1963), pp. 196ff., but the debate continues. It is interesting that thirty years ago some of the most vigorous defenders of the early dating of the Currency Decree and so on placed these at the time Mattingly now prefers. The latest assessment of the letter forms is by J. Barron, *Journal of Hellenic Studies*, 103 (1983), pp. 1ff.

[21]For comedy, a simpler problem, V. Ehrenberg, *The People of Aristophanes* (2nd ed.; Oxford, 1951), is a classic; M. Croiset, *Aristophanes and the Political Parties at Athens*, a sensitive study, has been reissued (new York, 1973).

ment.''[22]

For Athens we now have at last a solid, judicious treatment of the Athenian empire, and specialized studies on some organs of its government, though not in English of its assembly; it should be noted that a book first published by Boeckh in 1817 on the political economy of Athens still has great value, the oldest such study on any aspect of Greek history to which we can turn in more than antiquarian interest.[23] While Athens must remain the center of our attention, its place is often exaggerated; on the other hand there are far too many books entitled Greek democracy or Greek tragedy, as if these were general fruits of Hellenic culture rather than being rooted very specifically in Athenian life.

A useful advance in recent years has been the widening of geographical interest beyond Athens and Sparta; studies of many other *poleis* have been published, varying in value in part on the amount of evidence which is available.[24] Oddly enough Chalcis and Eretria as well as various states on the eastern shore of the Aegean remain almost untapped; for the latter at least we may have to wait for more field work. The western Greeks also have not had the attention they deserve; since Dunbabin's solid survey a great deal of archeological exploration has occurred, though in truth the western colonies cannot be said to have had major roles either politically or

[22]P. Roussel, *Sparte* (1960), remains the best general study; the latest treatments are by P. Cartledge (1979), J.T. Hooker (1980), L.T. Fitzhardinge (1980), but there will be more. M.I. Finley, *Problèmes de la guerre en Grèce ancienne,* ed. J.P. Vernant (Paris, 1968), pp. 143-60, shows that Sparta was not "militaristic" as we normally understand that term; J. Chambers, *The Historian,* 40 (1978), pp. 271-85, draws a useful distinction between the treatment and standing of Spartan and Messenian helots which helps explain why Brasidas could use helots *as hoplites;* on Spartan artistic abilities see the trenchant comments of R.M. Cook, *Classical Quarterly,* n.s. 12 (1962), pp. 156-58, and P. Janni, *La cultura di Sparta arcaica* (Rome 1968).

[23]R. Meiggs, *The Athenian Empire* (Oxford, 1971); A. Boeckh, *Die Staatshaushaltung der Athener,* 2 vols. (3rd ed.; Munich, 1886), with an English translation at Boston in 1857, a work totally ignored by H. Bengtson, *Introduction to Ancient History* (Berkeley, 1970). See also P.J. Rhodes, *The Athenian Boule* (Oxford, 1972); R.A. de Laix, *Probouleusis at Athens* (Berkeley, 1973); W. Robert Connor, *The New Politicians of Fifth-Century Athens* (Princeton, 1971). M.H. Hansen, *The Athenian Ecclesia* (Copenhagen, 1983), is a collection of specialized articles; he has published a more integrated work in German (1984).

[24]A list may be found in my *Individual and Community;* see also M. Amit, *Great and Small Poleis* (Brussels, 1973).

7

culturally despite their wealth.[25]

All of us nowadays detest imperialism; this dislike, as we shall see later, extends back to the Roman Empire. But amazingly the Athenian empire remains largely impervious to assault, though it ruthlessly exacted tribute — the proceeds of which are displayed in the well-known tribute lists — and interfered without mercy in the affairs of subject states.[26] Even a dedicated Marxist like Ste Croix can assert that the empire was popular among the subjects and in a magnificently buttressed book on the origins of the Peloponnesian War places the blame squarely on Sparta, though to do so he has to distort the bearing of the Megarian decree beyond all reason.[27] Pericles remains an Olympian leader; one might argue the contrary view that by encouraging the citizens to treat the allies as objects of exploitation he was basically responsible for the eventual collapse of Athenian power,[28] but thus far no one has dared to engage in a full-scale, critical treatment of Pericles' foreign and domestic policies. Were all Athenians as enthusiastic about bearing their political and military burdens as is suggested in his famous Funeral Oration? Burckhardt was not so sure: "The Periclean Age in Athens was in every sense of the word an age in which any peaceful and prudent citizen of our time would refuse to live."[29]

[25]T.J. Dunbabin, *The Western Greeks* (Oxford, 1948); M.I. Finley, *Ancient Sicily* (2d ed.; London, 1979). Archeological work is summarized in *Kokalos, Atti* of the several congresses of studies in Magna Graecia, etc.

[26]B.D. Merrit, H.T. Wade-Gery, and M.F. McGregor, *The Athenian Tribute Lists,* 4 vols. (Cambridge, Mass., 1939-53), a fundamental work comparable to A.W. Gomme et al., *Historical Commentary on Thucydides,* 5 vols. (Oxford, 1945-81). G.E. M. de Ste Croix treats Athenian legal interference in the subject states in *Classical Quarterly,* n.s. 11 (1961), pp.94-112 and 268-80.

[27]*The Origins of the Peloponnesian War* (London, 1972); *Historia,* 3 (1954), pp. 1-41, soon rebutted by Bradeen, Pleket, Quinn, and de Romilly, whose *Thucydides and Athenian Imperialism* (Oxford, 1963), is one of the most important recent studies of Thucydides.

[28]Typical of the weaknesses of our sources even for Athens is the fact that the ostracism in 443 of Thucydides, son of Melesias, perhaps the single most significant step in Athenian acceptance of empire, is known only from brief mention in Plutarch, *Pericles* 11-12, 14 (I am not convinced by A. Andrewes, *Journal of Hellenic Studies,* 98 [1978], pp. 1-8, who asserts Plutarch is "worthless".)

[29]J. Burckhardt, *Force and Freedom* (New York, 1943), ch. VI; in considering the Funeral Oration one must always keep in mind P. Stadter's demonstration in *The Speeches in Thucydides* (Chapel Hill, 1973), that though Plutarch knew it well he never cited it in his life of Pericles to illustrate Pericles' principles.

GREECE

It would be difficult to predict the future course of historical investigations in the fifth century. In many areas, as for example the question whether the "peace of Callias" really existed, scholars have been reduced to sifting through huge masses of articles and books to conclude that neither black nor white will suffice; a new interpretation must be a shade of gray between the two extremes. Genuine originality of views is more easily achieved for the formative era of Greek civilization or in the fourth century, but very possibly a genius will arise to revolutionize our understanding of fundamental factors affecting the fifth century. At the moment the best survey of the era is the thoughtful and rounded product of Will's pen, with excellent bibliographies for each chapter.[30]

The second volume of Will's survey is also the most recent extensive treatment of the fourth century, but this (by Mossé entirely) still gives the conventional picture of an era of gloom and decay after the glories of the age of Pericles.[31] Beginning with the intricacies of the Corinthian war, the states fought each other to total exhaustion by 362, when they lay in unconscious readiness to accept Macedonian rule. Internally, the *polis* world was riven by conflict of rich and poor, a problem illuminated by Aristotle in several books of the *Politics*. Loyalty to the ideals of the *polis* was corrupted by secular, materialistic ambition; men wished to hold public office continuously, "moved by the profits to be derived from office and the handling of public property."[32]

One must wonder whether we would draw this picture if we did not have the Aristotelian analysis and the dreary pages of that second-rate historian Xenophon. If the Oxyrhynchus historian or Ephorus had survived intact would the same view be dominant? Politically, for example, international strife had been endemic since the *poleis* emerged in the eighth century; as Plato commented, "Every city is in a natural state of war with every other, not indeed

[30]E. Will, *Le Monde grec et l'Orient* (Paris, 1972). The most idiosyncratic work in recent years in R. Sealey, *A History of the Greek City-States ca. 700-338 B.C.* (Berkeley, 1977), a strictly political narrative which judges the Great Rhetra not authentic and, after Beloch, considers Draco a snake; it has good discussion of the sources for each period.

[31]C. Mossé in E. Will et al,. *Le monde grec et l'Orient*, 2 (Paris, 1975). As Cartledge wryly comments, *Gnomon*, 50 (1978), p. 653, the idea of a crisis in the fourth century "ought not to become dogma," but it dominates the essays in *Hellenische Poleis*, ed. E.C. Welskopf, 4 vols. (Berlin, 1974).

[32]See *Politics* 3. 4. 6 (1279a. 13ff.).

proclaimed by heralds, but everlasting.''[33] Again, *stasis* had been an unfortunate consequence of the strife of noble factions from the days of Alcaeus and before, and one may doubt if it was really worse in the fourth century.[34] The basic fact, again, that the naval master in the Aegean and the ultimate arbiter of Greek politics, down to the rise of Philip, had been the Persian king is too often muffled.[35] It might have been wiser to exploit Greek divisiveness by asserting direct power, but the Persians perhaps had drawn lessons from the failure of Xerxes even if they thereby left the road open for Alexander. Here one may observe that the parallel picture of the Persian empire as one in decline is equally misleading; by the time of Alexander the Persian King of Kings had put down all revolts of satraps, Egypt, and elsewhere, which perhaps facilitated the Macedonian conquest, though the greatest general of antiquity had to fight *two* major battles to break Persian power (Sassanian and other Near Eastern empires fell after one defeat).

Even if there was not more internecine war than previously, conscious analysis of its affects was feasible in several respects. First, the conduct of war itself became professional on the level both of generals and of their mercenary followers, a development which has been explored in studies of Xenophon, the rise of peltasts, improvements in fortification and in siegecraft, and Athenian frontier defence policy.[36] The so-called *condottieri* generals who operated in Egypt and Asia Minor as far as the Persians permitted still warrant further investigation. Secondly, leading intellectuals such as Isocrates preached the need to mitigate warfare or even end it, an attitude aiming at a ''common peace,'' which perhaps weakened the will of

[33]*Laws* 626a. V. Martin, *La Vie internationale dans la Grèce des cités (VI-IV⁵ s. av. J.-C.* (Paris, 1940), emphasizes the anarchy of the *polis* world in a study too little noted because of its publication during the year of the collapse of France.

[34]See generally A.W. Lintott, *Violence, Civil Strife and Revolution in the Classical City* (London, 1982).

[35]See my essay on Greeks and Persians in the fourth century B.C., *Iranica Antiqua*, 11 (1976), pp. 61ff.; J.M. Cook, *The Persian Empire* (London, 1983); H. Bengston, *The Greeks and the Persians from the Sixth to the Fourth Centuries* (New York, 1968), p. 213, sums up the truth, ''The following decades of Greek history are an unrelieved display of Persian domination,'' whereas Mossé can see only Persian ''pretentions'' (p. 13) and decline (pp. 66ff.). S. Hornblower, *Mausolus* (Oxford, 1981), has an interesting analysis of the Persian system of control in the satrapies.

[36]J.K. Anderson, *Military Theory and Practice in the Age of Xenophon* (Berkeley, 1970); J.P. Best, *Thracian Peltasts* (Groningen, 1969); J. Ober, *Fortress Attica* (Leiden, 1985); J.F. Vernant, ed., *Problèmes de la guerre en Grèce ancienne* (Paris, 1968).

the Greeks to resist Macedonia.[37] Finally, political theory burgeoned in the hands of Plato and Aristotle, the former in particular seeking ways to turn back the clock and secure stability. This search also led to idealization of the "ancestral constitution" at Athens as well as theoretical constructions of an ideal state or open challenge to established sexual and dietary conventions.[38]

Trade and industry expanded in the fourth century at the Piraeus, now the center of Aegean activity, and also elsewhere, though Greek exports tended to disappear from western markets for reasons which have not yet been fully explored.[39] The growing wealth of at least a minority is attested by the increased amount of gold jewelry, rare in previous centuries; but we do not have the necessary information for quantified studies save for some aspects of temple building at Athens, Epidaurus, Eleusis, and Delphi.[40]

Periodization is a necessary tool in the marshalling of historical data, but it has its serious dangers; we may come to think everyone in the periods we construct had the same views, and that they are rigidly divided from the past and future. In regard to the fourth century, it has always been conventional to link it culturally to the fifth century and separate it completely from the Hellenistic era, a view resting unconsciously on the fact that the *poleis* apparently occupy the center of the stage down to Philip of Macedon.

This arrangement has come under proper attack. In sculpture the canon of the human body was altered, statues twisted and writhed in emotional expression. For the fifth century we have busts labelled Themistocles and Pericles, but they are simply idealized portraits; so too it can be observed that "Pericles in his actual person eludes us." During the fourth century the rendition of individuals was somewhat

[37]T.T.B. Ryder, *Koine Eirene* (London, 1965).

[38]A. Fuks, *The Ancestral Constitution* (London, 1953); P. Vidal-Naquet, *Journal of Hellenic Studies*, 98 (1978), pp. 132-41, has an interesting portrayal of the deliberate unconventionality of the Cynics and efforts to return to "the age of Cronus" — reminiscent of the upheavals in the 1960s.

[39]The introductory chapter of M.I. Rostovtzeff, *The Social and Economic History of the Hellenistic World* (Oxford, 1941), argues for a developing economic crisis but also produces evidence on expansion; A. French, *The Growth of the Athenian Economy* (London, 1964).

[40]R.A. Higgins, *Greek and Roman Jewelry* (2d ed.; London, 1980); H. Hoffmann and P.F. Davidson, *Greek Gold* (Brooklyn, 1965), mainly Hellenistic; A. Burford, *The Greek Temple Builders at Epidauros* (Liverpool, 1969).

realistic, and biography becomes more possible.[41] Public monies went for secular buildings rather than for temples; where temples were built the Corinthian capital was popular and columns were thinner and longer, a change paralleled by the revised canon of the human body in sculpture. Even in music Timotheus is said to have broken fifth-century sobriety and expressed the struggle at Salamis so that one could almost feel the splashes of oars and din of battle. Philosophically it has become clearer in recent discussions that the great Hellenistic evaluations of how a man should live were directly rooted in post-Socratic logical analysis and sweeping vision.[42]

Many would judge Plato the greatest thinker of the century (though Karl Popper might not agree), but certainly Isocrates has had the widest influence on many generations of writers and students. He did much to set a supple, balanced prose style which remained powerful on into the nineteenth century; a wealth of polished oratory survives from suits in the Athenian law courts, admirable sources for much of the social and economic life of the age. As a companion development Isocrates along with Aristotle and others consolidated the values and structure of aristocratic education in a mold which endured an equal length of time; this topic has been masterfully treated by Marrou in a book which ranks as one of the most important explorations of any ancient topic.[43]

These varied achievements scarcely warrant a pessimistic judgment of decline in Greek civilization and political life. If men had a more secular attitude, it was nonetheless the citizen levies of Athens and Thebes — not mercenaries — which were inspired by Demosthenes to stand shoulder by shoulder at Chaeronea.[44] Although Philip won the battle his victory was by no means inevitable. For Philip himself we now can rely on a powerful biography, exploring in vivid

[41]M. Bowra, *Periclean Athens* (London, 1971), p. 78; A. Momigliano, *Greek Biography* (Cambridge, Mass., 1971).

[42]Examples of these changes are B.R. Brown, *Anticlassicism in Greek Sculpture of the Fourth Century B.C.* (New York, 1973); A.W. Lawrence, *Greek Architecture* (3d ed., Penguin, 1973); A.A. Long, *Hellenistic Philosophy* (London, 1974).

[43]H.I. Marrou, *A History of Education in Antiquity* (Mentor paperback, 1964).

[44]Demosthenes deserves much more study; Badian promises a revision of his Martin lectures on the subject. His ability was appreciated by Adlai Stevenson: "Do you remember that in classical times when Cicero had finished speaking, the people said, 'How well he spoke' — but when Demosthenes had finished speaking, people said, 'Let us march'." (T.H. White, *The Making of the President 1968* [New York, 1969], p. 87). Others have not been so complimentary.

prose his skillful exploitation of Greek political divisions.[45] The wealth of literary sources and the considerable increase in epigraphic and numismatic evidence make the fourth century as a whole an era which will repay investigations across many areas in the future.

If we look generally at main currents in the treatment of Greek history one of the most obvious changes has been the general rejection of the nineteenth-century idealization of the Greeks, and especially of the Athenians, as embodiments of reasons. As a Black Power spokesman said, "We are told that Western Civilization begins with the Greeks, and that the epitome of that is Alexander the Great. The only thing that I can remember about Alexander the Great was that at age twenty-six he wept because there were no other people to kill, murder, and plunder. And that is the epitome of Western Civilization."[46] Ancient historians are not likely to go so far, but few of us would endorse the glowing picture of Periclean Athens recently presented by Bowra.[47] The book of decisive importance in this respect was Dodds' Sather lectures; the Regius professor of Greek boldly adduced psychological and anthropological theories and evidence to demonstrate the irrational side of Greek civilization.[48] In this approach, true, he had been preceded by his mentor Murray and others, but Dodd's pages remain powerful, if sometimes too sweeping. Magical practices, healing cults, and mysticism become more evident in the fourth century, and perhaps enjoyed a greater vogue then, but already in Hesiod's day one took a new pot to the village expert to be blessed.[49]

As idealization has waned so too has interest in the upper classes. Exploitation of the lower orders is now a more common theme, and there are efforts to explore the mind and behavior of "the silent majority," a favorite theme in contemporary history. A valuable

[45]G.T. Griffith, in N.G.L. Hammond and Griffith, *History of Macedonia*, 2 (Oxford, 1979).

[46]E. Cleaver in *The Dialect of Liberation*, ed. D. Cooper (Penguin, 1968), p. 154, quoted by K.J. Dover, *The Greeks* (Austin, Texas, 1981), pp. 8-9.

[47]Bowra, *Periclean Athens*; W. Jaeger, *Paideia*, 3 vols. (Berlin, 1936-55), a work which now appears aged. Let me note here that for the student who knows nothing about Greece H.D.F. Kitto, *The Greeks* (Penguin, 1951), and A. Andrewes, *The Greeks* (New York, 1967), still stand out among a wealth of general treatments.

[48]E.R. Dodds, *The Greeks and the Irrational* (Beacon paperback, 1957);but one must keep in mind as counterpoint B. Snell, *The Discovery of the Mind: The Greek Origins of European Thought* (Cambridge, Mass., 1953).

[49]D. Sabbatucci, *Saggio sul misticismo greco* (Rome, 1965); the short study by H.J. Rose of *Primitive Culture in Greece* (London, 1925).

study in this area is Ste Croix's massive, well-buttressed but eventually flawed discussion of class struggle, which will recur in my last chapter.[50] The variety of themes which have been the subject of discussion in this generation is amazing; one development has been the liberation of Greek homosexuality from its Victorian closet. True, Bethe published in 1907 a learned article on "die dorische Knabenliebe" (the adjective is an interesting distortion), but only recently have we had full-scale treatments of the topic in several languages for fairly general audiences.[51]

On the theoretical level the most important changes have come not from the application of Marxist concepts, vigorous though attention has been to Greek history in Russia (and also in Japan), but for western scholars the major vivifying force in recent studies lies in the exploration of anthropological theories or models and the drawing of comparisons with modern simple societies. This is not altogether new: W.S. Ferguson wrote an interesting essay on the death rites of Zulu and Spartan kings, and Grote noted parallels between the initiation of Mandan Indians and Spartan youth.[52] Still, we may agree with an eminent scholar that anthropology is "the most influential of the social sciences" as far as history is concerned.[53] Nor is this surprising. Students in both disciplines consider man in virtually every aspect of his manifold activities; both tend to draw deductions from simple observation and even to rely upon intuition; abler scholars in both fields on occasion write broad syntheses.

This interest in anthropology has often helped to raise questions and to point out the direction in which solutions may be sought, but it must always be remembered that anthropological data do not in themselves *prove* anything in Greek history.[54] The seductive appeal

[50]G.E.M. de Ste Croix, *The Class Struggle in the Ancient Greek World* (London, 1981).

[51]When I was a graduate student the only studies available were E. Bethe's essay in *Rheinisches Museum* and "Hans Licht," *Sittengeschichte Griechenlands*, 2 vols. (Dresden, 1925-28); note that the author, Paul Brandt, felt it desirable to use a pseudonym. See now K.J. Dover, *Greek Homosexuality* (London, 1978); H. Patzer, *Die griechischen Knabenliebe* (Wiesbaden, 1982); F. Bouffiere, *Eros adolescent* (Paris, 1980; *non vidi*). Perhaps the most remarkable essay in this line is Martin Kilmer on genital phobia, *Journal of Hellenic Studies*, 102 (1982), pp. 104ff.

[52]W.S. Ferguson, "The Zulus and the Spartans," *Harvard African Studies*, 2 (1918), pp. 197-234; Grote, II, chap. vi.

[53]Lawrence Stone, *Past and Present*, 85 (1979), pp. 13-14.

[54]In *Individual and the Community* I have discussed two anthropological models on the origins of states which help determine the probable course of development in early Greece.

may easily go too far; anthropologist make much of the role of kinship, but it is a wisp of the imagination for Greek history from Homeric times onward.[55] As Finley observed, for Radcliffe-Brown, "the conduct of individuals to one another is very largely regulated on the basis of kinship . . . This is no description of the world of Odysseus, in which the family tie, though strong, was narrowly defined" and the personal ties of leaders and followers were basic.[56] Always in works emphasizing kinship the role of *genos* has been stressed, but even the existence of *gene* in Greece has been largely exploded.[57]

In recent scholarship two vigorous schools of view have emerged which are based on anthropology, social psychology, and kindred disciplines. One is largely located in Paris and draws upon Gernet, Levy-Strauss, Braudel, Meyerson, and others to produce works with such exotic titles as *The Gardens of Adonis* or *The Black Hunter*. Yet, as Walcot notes, "We must at least introduce our students to the work currently being undertaken by the French structuralists, however daunting a prospect this may be to some,"[58] for these studies of intellectual and mythological threads sometimes throw unexpected light on Greek institutions and beliefs.

The other approach is shared by English scholars and some Europeans, who have concentrated on socio-economic aspects. The result virtually is a new orthodoxy which can be applied to all fields of ancient history but is perhaps more visible in the simpler Greek world than in the vast and complicated Roman Empire. Three strands in this point of view deserve notice. First, the question as to how we

---

[55]R.J. Littman, *Ancient Society*, 10 (1979), pp. 5-31, goes farthest in finding political effects; S.C. Humphreys, *Anthropology and the Greeks* (London, 1978), would like to dwell on the role of kinship but notes (p. 198) that "political procedures developed in Greece at the expense of kinship."

[56]*World of Odysseus*, p. 78 in first edition; in rev. ed., p. 105, where Finley spends more time on kinship but largely on the household level. In *Politics in the Ancient World* (Cambridge, 1983), kinship does not appear in the index.

[57]F. Bourriot, *Recherches sur la nature du genos* (Paris, 1976).

[58]P. Walcot, *Journal of Hellenic Studies*, 103 (1983), p. 193, reviewing *Myth, Religion and Society: Structuralist Essays*, by M. Detienne and others (Cambridge, 1981). Other examples are J.P. Vernant, *Myth and Society in Ancient Greece* (London, 1982); M. Detienne, *The Gardens of Adonis* (London, 1977); M. Detienne and J.P. Vernant, *Cunning Intelligence in Greek Culture and Society* (Hassocks, 1978); P. Vidal-Naquet, *Le chasseur noir* (Paris, 1981; English translation, Baltimore, 1986). Predecessors include H. Jeanmaire, *Couroi et Courètes* (Lille, 1939); L. Gernet, *The Anthropology of Ancient Greece* (Baltimore, 1982).

evaluate the general level of economic life. Earlier in this century Meyer and Rostovtzeff in particular assessed the Greek economic structure as a complex system with extensive commercial and industrial sectors. This was fiercely attacked by Hasebroek; nowadays Finley, Humphreys, and many others agree that the ancient economy was primitive. The agricultural sector was dominant, and trade restricted essentially to luxury items for the upper classes; in the earlier centuries of Greek history, as noted earlier, one should think rather of gift exchange than a true search for profit. As a consequence states had little interest in economic matters, or conversely financial and other economic sectors did not have that influence on public policy which we assume automatically for modern times. Secondly, ancient cities were parasitical centers of consumption for the most part, a view derived from Max Weber's study of east German towns. And finally the socio-economic side of life was predominant over political interests.

We need not grant too easily acceptance of this attractive, well integrated approach, dominant though it is in many quarters.[59] Here it may be noted briefly that trade in commodities such as wool, timber, stone, grain, and other bulk items *was* active. As we shall see when we come to the political role of equestrians in the Roman Republic, it is all too easy to exaggerate their influence, but it will not do to deny *any* interest by Greek *poleis* in industry and commerce. Harbor works such as those of Themistocles at the Piraeus, true, were undertaken largely for naval purposes,[60] but the striking of copper coinage for market purposes, the care taken by Athens to obtain treaties with Thracian and other monarchs to safeguard its grain supply, and other testimony to interrelations of political and economic spheres cannot be overlooked. Simplicity in structure can be conjoined with sophistication in practice as Thompson has shown in several thoughtful essays.[61]

[59]Besides those already named, K. Hopkins, M.M. Austin, H.W. Pleket, and others tend in great or lesser degree to share the views just described; one of their major roots can be traced back to Sir Henry Maine, *Ancient Law* (1861) and Fustel de Coulanges, *La cité antique*, 1864.

[60]But note R.M. Cook's firm view, *Journal of Hellenic Studies*, 99 (1979), pp. 152-3, that the *diolkos* across the isthmus of Corinth was constructed primarily for commercial reasons; on the other hand, Jeffery, *Archaic Greece*, repeatedly overemphasizes the role of "trade."

[61]W.I. Thompson, *De Hagniae hereditate* (Leiden, 1976); *L'Antiquité classique*, 51 (1982), pp. 53-85, a direct challenge to oversimplifications by the "primitivist" school.

GREECE

Secondly, Athens and other major Greek cities had to import grain to feed their urban population, and this import had to be covered by exports, i.e., the production of saleable items. The rapid spread of cities in Greece can scarcely be explained except as a consequence of their productive and distributive functions in a vibrant economy, supported by the expansion of commercial and industrial elements which were tied to colonization and the resulting overseas demand for Greek products. And finally an essay by Rahe shows clearly that Athenian citizens were involved directly in the political processes of their community; indeed, "the concerns that were primary were not social, they were political."[62]

In sum, the study of Greek history has been enlivened and conventional views seriously challenged. We cannot discard the classics of the past, though admitting that too often they have been concentrated on fifth-century Athens; but our scope both chronologically and geographically must now be far broader. Any student should also keep an eye on recent trends, but he need not accept any argument simply because it has been presented forcefully, even at times dogmatically.

[62]P.A. Rahe, *American Historical Review*, 89 (1984), pp. 265-93; much the same view is expressed at greater length by C. Meier, *Die Entstehung des Politischen bei den Griechen* (Frankfurt, 1980). See also E. Ruschenbusch, *Untersuchungen zur Staat und Politik in Griechenland vom 7.-4. Jh v. Chr.* (Bamberg, 1978). V. Ehrenberg, *The Greek State* (2d ed.; London,; 1974), remains a work of major utility.

II

THE HELLENISTIC AGE

"More than any other period of ancient history, perhaps more than any other period in the general history of our 'western world,' the Hellenistic age is near to our own" in many fundamental characteristics; but it is, alas, the most difficult era in all ancient history to reconstruct in a meaningful account.[1] The leading history of the period, that of Polybius, survives after the first five books only in fragments, and in any case his objective was to explain the rise of Rome to his fellow Greeks.[2] For the rest we rely on Justin's abridgement of Pompeius Trogus, the limited and sometimes partisan information in Josephus, and sundry scraps. Archeologically Hellenistic levels of major cities such as Alexandria and Antioch have not been easy to excavate, and even for lesser centers Roman remains are often predominant save especially at Delos. Epigraphic evidence is valuable for areas on or close to the Aegean, but far less so for Syria or Egypt, where papyri become important.[3] Numismatic material is abundant, and royal coin portraits are realistic to the point that we can even diagnose thyroid problems.[4]

The international politics of the age, moreover, were highly complicated in a web of marriages, alliances, and contentions which produced no less than six Syrian wars between the Ptolemies and Seleucids, as intricate as were the relations of European powers in the

[1]Will, *Le monde grec et l'Orient*, 2, p. 643; cf. the rueful comment by the eminent historian of modern Germany, G. Barraclough, *History in a Changing World* (Oxford, 1955), p. 217, that Bismarck now is a Neolithic figure and we will gain more light "by studying the life and times of Alexander the Great." The judicious *Histoire politique du monde hellénistique* by E. Will, 2 vols. (2d ed.; Nancy, 1982), cites virtually all relevant literature; a briefer treatment by Will is in *Cambridge Ancient History*, 7.1 (Cambridge, 1984). C. Schneider, *Kulturgeschichte der Hellenismus*, 2 vols. (Munich, 1967-69), treats all aspects. See also C. Preaux, *Le monde hellénistique*, 2 vols. (Paris, 1978). In English W.W. Tarn and G.T. Griffith, *Hellenistic Civilization* (3d ed.; London, 1952) is a more rounded and solid treatment than various more recent surveys.

[2]F.W.Walbank, *Polybius* (Berkeley, 1972), and his *Historical Commentary on Polybius*, 3 vols. (Oxford, 1957-79).

[3]Unfortunately inscriptions are widely scattered in publication; see C.B. Welles, *Royal Correspondence in the Hellenistic Period* (New Haven, 1934), and the useful collection in translation by S.M. Burstein (Cambridge, 1985).

[4]N. Davis and C.M. Kraay, *The Hellenistic Kingdoms: Portrait Coins and History* (London, 1973). Note how deliberately the obesity of Ptolemy VIII Physcon was emphasized; down through the nineteenth century it was fatness, not thinness, which was desirable.

early modern period. Nonetheless we cannot ignore the Hellenistic period for at least three major reasons. Political and cultural developments had lasting effects on Rome; the background for Christianity lies in the era; and in itself it is a fascinating example of colonial imperialism. The first two aspects have been often studied; the third still demands more intensive analysis, and I shall return to this issue later. But in general it remains true that "modern research on the history of the Hellenistic age has not been blessed with historical monographs."[5]

Consideration of the Hellenistic age must begin with the awe-inspiring yet puzzling figure, Alexander the Great. There are two recent surveys in English of the literature, and new studies continue to proliferate.[6] Until recently the picture drawn by Tarn of an idealistic dreamer seeking to unite East and West has been attractive and underlies the popular novels of Mary Renault.[7] (I have always visualized Tarn as sitting in his study by an often misty Scottish loch, imbibing a local product, and diverting himself by composing for his grandchildren fairy tales, one of which was published; it was comforting to have David Stronach, who once lived in Tarn's house, confirm at least the loch and mist.) Badian, however, has been steadily chipping away at Tarn's picture and turns Alexander into a ruthless Realpolitiker; for Schachermeyr Alexander is "ein Unmensch, ein Tyran."[8]

Why the diversity? In part it is the consequence of the limited ability of the academic mind to understand the uniqueness of great generals who have their own wellsprings of action, but difficulties also arise from the paucity of solid evidence. The much later works of

---

[5]E. Olshausen, *Gnomon*, 48 (1976), p. 461.

[6]E. Badian, *Classical World*, 65 (1971), pp. 37-56, 77-83; J. Rufus Fears, *American Historical Review*, 82 (1977), pp. 1220-23; in German, J. Seiberg, *Alexander der Grosse* (Darmstadt, 1972), is even more inclusive. G.T. Griffith, *Alexander: The Main Problems* (Cambridge, 1966), contains Tarn's famous lecture on Alexander as creating the theory of the brotherhood of man, Badian's critique, and other useful essays.

[7]It is interesting that neither Badian nor any one else ever cites a two-part article by M. Fisch, *American Journal of Philology*, 58 (1937), pp. 59ff., 129ff., though Fisch was a Stoic specialist who calmly disproved Tarn's theory. Valuable work sometimes sinks without a trace in later literature.

[8]Badian is revising and assembling his articles, published in many journals; F. Schachermeyr, *Alexander der Grosse* (Vienna, 1973); the best effort to portray Alexander as rational remains R. Andreotti, *Historia* 1 (1950), pp. 583ff., 5 (1956), pp. 257ff.; *Saeculum* 8 (1957), pp. 120ff. (K. Kraft's posthumous *Der "rationale" Alexander* [Kallmünz, 1971] has serious weaknesses).

Arrian, Curtius Rufus, and others themselves provide very contrasting interpretations, and their use of earlier sources still gives rise to argument.[9] The decrees and letters preserved epigraphically throw very little light.[10] More valuable is the massive coinage, which shows first that Alexander deliberately flooded the western satrapies with standardized tetradrachms and drachmas from many mints and then secondly that after Babylon the coinage became far less regular, including a remarkable eight-drachma piece showing Alexander on horseback attacking an enemy on an elephant (Porus?) — further testimony that in the eastern satrapies Alexander's views changed greatly and perhaps erratically.[11] Amazingly enough truly new light has been shed on the timing and routes of Alexander's advance as dictated by weather conditions and availability of water and food.[12] There can be hope that if Alexander himself remains a testing problem for any historian we may be able to see more clearly his activities in the eastern satrapies.

Among the successor dynasties the Seleucids rarely receive the attention which they deserve, for their realm was the linchpin of the Hellenistic world. The extensive program of colonization, which has been carefully surveyed, helped to place a Hellenic stamp on the Near and Middle East down to Arab and even Turkish times;[13] at the site of one such colony, Dura Europos, the ground plan and some of the initial stages of occupation are visible, through most of the valuable Dura remains are of the Roman period.

In part this neglect reflects the tendency to approach the Seleucids from the point of view of Rome or the Jews. The best biography of any Seleucid ruler, that of Antiochus IV by Mørkholm, is widely

[9]Plutarch's life now has a commentary by J.R. Hamilton (Oxford, 1969); for Arrian see P. Brunt's recent Loeb edition, P.A. Stadter, *Arrian of Nicomedia* (Chapel Hill, 1980); A.R. Bosworth, *Historical Commentary on Arrian's History of Alexander*, 1 (Oxford, 1980).

[10]This material is collected by A.J. Heisserer, *Alexander the Great and the Greeks* (Norman, 1980).

[11]Thus far one must rely on A.R. Bellinger, *Essays on the Coinage of Alexander the Great* (New Haven, 1963); M. Thompson, *Alexander's Drachm Mints* (New York, 1983); and for the eastern coinage Dürr, *Schweizer Münzblätter*, 24 (1974), pp. 33f. On Alexander's effort to introduce *proskynesis* it may be observed that this ritual did not involve prostration, as is almost always assumed; see E.J. Bickerman, *Parola del Passato* 18 (1963), pp. 241-55, or R.N. Frye, *Iranica Antiqua*, 9 (1972), pp. 102-7.

[12]D.W. Engels, *Alexander the Great and the Logistics of the Macedonian Army* (Berkeley, 1978).

[13]G.M. Cohen, *The Seleucid Colonies* (Wiesbaden, 1978); the other end of the story is surveyed by S. Vryonis, *The Decline of Medieval Hellenism in Asia Minor* (Berkeley, 1971).

rounded, and takes up in detail events on the troubled eastern frontier;[14] the stages of deterioration here are the most visible markers of the decline of the Hellenistic state system. Yet in most general accounts the memorable part of his reign is his policy in Palestine, which led to the revolution of the Maccabees. In later pages we shall consider again the relations of Judaism and Hellenism, but it may be pointed out that the earlier theory that Antiochus IV was promoting "a well-defined domestic policy aiming at the introduction of Greek culture throughout his realm" has been generally discarded.[15]

Another problem in recreating Seleucid history and the structure of its government is the inadequacy of sources, both literary and epigraphic. There are valuable edicts and letters to various cities, but almost entirely for the western districts fronting on the Aegean; as one moves eastward this type of material shoals off rapidly, though one can see at least some dimensions of the important city of Susa.[16] From Seleucus himself onward the kings established a position for themselves which it is now felt owed very little, except in trappings, to earlier Persian patterns: "It is not the custom of the Persians and other peoples that I [Seleucus I] impose upon you but that which is common to all, that what is decreed by the king is always just."[17] The internal organization of the vast Seleucid realm, however, cannot be described in sufficient detail to detect local variations.[18]

A great deal, nonetheless, may be feasible in the future. The Seleucids struck voluminous coinage, which helped turn at least urban centers away from the natural economy characteristic of the Persian system; this source has by no means been completely explored. Russian surveys and the French excavations at Ai Khanoum (Alexandria Oxiana perhaps), unlikely to resume soon, have thrown bright light on the continuing hellenization of eastern settlements, which is also visible in the Greco-Indian coinage.[19]

---

[14]O. Mørkholm, *Antiochus IV of Syria* (Copenhagen, 1966).

[15]Mørkholm, p. 138; cf. T. Fischer, *Seleukiden und Makkabäer* (Bochum, 1980).

[16]G. Le Rider, *Suse sous les Séleucides et les Parthes* (Paris, 1965).

[17]Appian, *Syrian Wars* 61.

[18]The brevity of E. Bickerman's still standard *Institutions des Séleucides* (Paris, 1933), illustrates the paucity of evidence; one aspect is treated by H. Bengston, *Die Strategie in der hellenistischer Zeit*, 2 (2d ed.; Munich, 1964). H. Kreissig surveys *Wirtschaft und Gesellschaft im Seleukidenreich* (Berlin, 1978).

[19]G. Woodcock, *The Greeks in India* (London, 1966), is a sober successor to Tarn's great flight of fancy, *The Greeks in Bactria and India* (3d ed. by F.L. Holt; Chicago, 1985). See also A.K. Narain, *The Indo-Greeks* (Oxford, 1957), and the essays collected by F. Altheim and J. Rehark, *Der Hellenismus in Mittelasien* (Darmstadt, 1969).

Unfortunately Parthian history and art continue to invite little attention, but improvement in this respect may be hoped from colleagues in Near Eastern history.[20] As remains true for the Roman Empire, cultural and political cross-currents between the Greco-Roman *oikoumene* and Eastern cultures are far more important – and two-sided – than is often recognized.

The second major dynasty, that of the Ptolemies, is much better known in all respects. Literary evidence is relatively abundant, especially for the first rulers of the line, whose glories were celebrated in fulsome poetry; we even have such intimate details as Callixenus' description (preserved in Athenaeus 5. 196ff.) of the great procession for the Ptolemeia of 271/0 (though this can be paralleled for the Seleucids in Polybius' account [30. 25-26] of the celebration of the games at Daphne by Antiochus IV).[21] One testimony to the wealth of sources is the recent publication of a long and very detailed study of Ptolemaic Alexandria, though this great city was always distinct from the Egyptian countryside and at times specifically distinguished in the later Roman term as Alexandria ad Aegyptum. Fraser, however, can lead one astray; at times one will learn more about the Ptolemies themselves from another recent publication simply of portraits of the rulers.[22]

Politically an intensive study of the evidence soon dispels a common view of the Ptolemaic administration as highly structured and governed by well-defined principles under "one of the most rigidly centralized bureaucracies that the world has ever seen."[23] There were indeed precise regulations covering the production of many commodities, yet the papyri demonstrate that rules were made to be thwarted by bribery and self-seeking officials. What obtained for the Fayum, moreover, was not necessarily the practice of upper Egypt, the Thebaid, which always stood in a separate position.[24] The fact that financial officials ranked low on the scale of Ptolemaic titles

---

[20]M.A.R. Colledge has recently done his best with *Parthian Art* (Ithaca, 1977), and *The Parthians* (New York, 1967); K. Schippman gives a terse summary in *Grundzüge der parthischen Geschichte* (Darmstadt, 1980).

[21]On the important role of Arsinoe in relation to her brother Ptolemy II see L. Longega, *Arsinoe II* (Padua, 1965).

[22]P.M. Fraser, *Ptolemaic Alexandria*, 2 vols. (Oxford, 1972); H. Kyrieleis, *Bildnisse der Ptolemäer* (Berlin, 1975).

[23]A.H.M. Jones, *Cities of the Eastern Roman Provinces* (Oxford, 1937), p. 298. The rules are collected in M.T. Lenger, *Corpus des ordonnances des Ptolémées* (Brussels, 1964).

[24]J.D. Thomas, *The Ptolemaic Epistrategos* (Opladen, 1975).

has recently been brought to light;[25] the Ptolemies thought more consciously about foreign policies and problems, and simply expected the system of rents, taxes, and labor dues to produce the grain and cash needed for these objectives. As is well known, the internal administration deteriorated in the second and first centuries, and so too Ptolemaic activity declined. Long before its demise the dynasty was upheld only by intermittent Roman support (which at times yielded great profits to Roman politicians and generals);[26] the glowing picture painted by Tarn of the efforts of Cleopatra (the only Ptolemaic ruler who could speak the native Egyptian tongue) to restore true independance must be heavily discounted.[27]

Whereas numismatic and epigraphical scholars often produce essays which do not exactly scintillate, students of papyri, working from testimony of actual life, rarely are dull; the vigorous papers by my former colleague Youtie as well as the reconstruction of plays by Menander from the smallest of scraps by Turner illustrate the varied skills of papyrologists.[28] Socially and economically there are many questions still to be put which may produce unexpected answers; Hopkins, for example, has upset a cardinal principle of anthropological theory that brothers and sisters do not marry by demonstrating that this was a common practice in Egypt.[29] One problem in handling papyri, though, is not likely to be resolved soon; apart from the Zenon archive and a few other examples, papyri are usually published by collections, and an over-all index lies far in the future.

The Antigonid dynasty is often placed on a par with the Seleucids and Ptolemies, a position not warranted had it not often been in control of the ancestral home of Hellenic civilization. Philip V was the first ruler to suffer from Roman expansion eastward, and Macedonia caused the Romans more protracted difficulty than any

[25]L. Mooren, *La hierarchie de cour ptolémaïque* (Louvain, 1977), points out that the *dioecetes* himself ranked lower than the strategus of the Arsinoite nome down to 120.

[26]Dissertations on Roman relations to Egypt have been written by E. Bloedow (Würzburg, 1963), H. Heinen (Tübingen, 1968), E. Olshausen (Erlangen, 1963), and an older study by H. Winkler (Leipzig, 1933).

[27]So too the cerebral relationship of Caesar and Cleopatra drawn by G.B. Shaw is misleading; as is often the case Shakespeare had keener intuition. See H. Volkmann, *Cleopatra* (London, 1958).

[28]H.C. Youtie, *Scriptiunculae*, 2 vols. (Amsterdam, 1973; Bonn, 1981); E.G. Turner, *The Papyrologist at Work* (Durham, 1973), who also has a useful introduction to papyri, *Greek Papyri* (2d ed.; Oxford, 1980). F. Cumont, *L'Egypte des astrologues* (Brussels, 1937), illustrates what a wide range of evidence could be usefully deployed.

[29]K. Hopkins, *Comparative Studies in Society and History*, 22 (1980), pp. 303-54.

other Hellenistic state. The fierce debate which still swirls about the "Macedonian" wars will be considered in relation to the Roman Republic, but one must here at least point out the thorough study by Gruen, which gives a full treatment of the complexities of the Hellenistic system on the political level and is well buttressed by a wealth of detailed references to sources and modern literature.[30] As for the Greeks themselves, various problems concerning the Achaean and Aetolian leagues have been settled – or at least thoroughly ventilated – by Aymard, Larsen, and Moretti. If there was a good deal of social unrest, again tied to the Roman interference, studies of such tensions in modern times should lead one to question the frequent assumption that in Hellenistic Greece this is conclusive testimony to a dreary decline, though after the Chremonidean war Athens itself sank into a backwater.[31]

The fact that Macedonia also had northern borders, facing rather uncivilized tribes, is now being explored more carefully by Adams, Borza, and the late Dell together with Greek and other colleagues in symposia at Thessalonica. Otherwise attention to Macedonia has largely been expressed in terms of biographies of some of its rulers; we must look forward more generally to the third volume of Hammond's history of Macedonia.[32]

Around the greater dynasties stretched an intricate tissue of small kingdoms and independent *poleis*, which helped to make Hellenistic politics as complicated as those of early modern Europe before the national states of Germany and Italy had crystallized. One of these, the Attalid dynasty of Pergamum, has had a great deal of attention;[33]

---

[30]E.S. Gruen, *The Hellenistic World and the Coming of Rome*, 2 vols. (Berkeley, 1984).

[31]J.A.O. Larsen, *Greek Federal States* (Oxford, 1968), gives full references on the leagues. Though aged, the classic by W.S. Ferguson, *Hellenistic Athens* (London, 1911), can still be described in Will's words as "précieux." See also P. MacKendrick, *Athenian Aristocracy, 399-71 B.C.* (Cambridge, Mass., 1969). On social unrest see chap. 3 below.

[32]In recent years the Greek government, spurred by Karamanlis (born in the north), has sought to eradicate any idea that *ancient* Macedonians and Greeks were different. This has led to one effort to get an encyclopedia to rewrite relevant articles as well as the slant of the touring exhibit, The Search for Alexander. Another example of the dangerous tendency to distort ancient history for modern purposes must suffice: the eulogy of Gaul by a patriotic if sometimes misguided Frenchman, J. Carcopino, *Les Etapes de l'impérialisme romain* (Paris 1961) (to explain the adjective Carcopino served as Minister of Education in the Vichy Government).

[33]E.V. Hansen, *The Attalids of Pergamum* (2d ed.; Ithaca, 1971); R.E. Allen, *The Attalid Kingdom* (Oxford, 1983); R.B. McShane, *The Foreign Policy of the Attalids of Pergamum* (Urbana, 1964).

most of the rest have languished in undue obscurity. The Nabataeans of the southern fringe have recently been discussed; but neither the Greek cities of south Russia nor the Bosporus have had the attention in Western languages which they deserve.[34] There are also the kingdoms of Asia Minor which call for study, especially now that their linguistic patterns are becoming clearer; the best biography of Mithridates, the wily foe of Rome who incited the Aegean in desperate revolt, is almost a century old. Cultural and religious developments in Asia Minor were rich in diversity; far too often the continuing influence of Iranian sources in the area is ignored. Would it be going too far to suggest that the bubbling vigor of Christianity in Asia Minor, when it becomes visible in the third and fourth centuries after Christ, rests on this pagan substructure?

International relations among these states took place, as I noted earlier, within a context of dynastic marriages, a great deal of war, and skillful diplomacy presented in polished rhetoric; commercial factors also played a role made manifest especially in the gifts of grain by several states to Rhodes, the entrepot of the eastern Mediterranean, after its severe earthquake in 227/6. There has been some discussion of royal marriages,[35] and warfare by land has had a good deal of treatment as in the special topics of elephants and mercenaries; a general study of the place of war in Hellenistic world would be useful.[36] Naval history has been less fully surveyed, except in some battles. Although it is not certain that we have enough evidence to go much beyond the building of behemoth galleys, the significant role of piracy deserves a more recent treatment than that of Ormerod.[37] Oddly enough diplomacy on the dynastic level has aroused little interest, but it is only a few years ago that a monograph was published on diplomacy in classical times.

Let us turn to more general problems arising from Hellenistic history, for some of these help to justify the stress on its importance

[34]P.C. Hammond, *The Nabataeans* (Lund, 1973); G. Vitucci, *Il regno di Bitinia* (Rome, 1953); D. Magie, *Roman Rule in Asia Minor*, 2 vols. (Princeton, 1950), is more encompassing than its title suggests and is abundantly documented.

[35]See the second chapter in L. Vatin, *Recherches sur le mariage et la condition de la femme mariée à l'époque hellénistique* (Paris, 1970).

[36]Apart from the well-known works by Tarn, Griffith, Scullard, B. Bar Kochva, *The Seleucid Army* (London, 1976), must be used with caution.

[37]H.A. Ormerod, *Piracy in the Ancient World* (Liverpool, 1924; reprint 1967); see the references under Seeraub in *Der Kleine Pauly*. Braudel's massive work on the Mediterranean in the sixteenth century offers suggestive parallels.

for modern historians suggested in the opening lines of this chapter. There has been, for instance, heated debate over the causes of the deterioration of European power in the twentieth century, and some anti-American participants in the argument have drawn a parallel with the Hellenistic world by suggesting that *its* decline also was the result of outside intrusion, in this case by brutal, uncivilized Romans. This point of view has been held by an number of ancient historians; in the gloomy days after the defeat of Germany in World War I Meyer deliverd in the preface to a revised edition of his study of Caesar and Pompey a harsh attack on the *Barbarei* which had crushed his noble country – though not named, the United States was, I am sure, in his mind. Residence for a year at the University of Illinois before the war apparently did not endear Americans to him.[38] Certainly the menace of Rome sapped the independence of Hellenistic states; as Attalus II reported a debate of his council it was deemed too dangerous "to launch an undertaking without their participation."[39] Yet most scholars justly feel that the roots of Hellenistic decline were internal, in the increasing reluctance of subjects to support the great monarchies.[40]

Nowadays, to turn to another aspect, it is not considered proper to praise Rostovtzeff, whose conceptual framework is considered weak, leading to "vagueness and inadequacy" in the treatment of Hellenistic peasants for example.[41] The trouble rather is the fact that he brought with him to the United States "bourgeois" attitudes fostered in Czarist St. Petersburg which are now out of favor; but the greatness of his work on the Hellenistic era cannot be denied. He was master of as great a range of information as anyone who has worked on the period, visible not only in the notes which occupy his third volume but also in the commentary on the plates – and those illustrations, we must remember, were not incidental decorations of the text but fundamental supports to his arguments. For Rostovtzeff, however, the Roman Empire marked the high point of ancient economic activity, whereas Heichelheim preferred the centuries after

[38]E. Meyer, *Caesars Monarchie und das Principat des Pompejus* (2d ed.; Stuttgart, 1919).
[39]Welles, *Royal Correspondence*, no. 61.
[40]F. De Martino, *Storia economica di Roma antica*, 1 (Florence, 1979), pp. 210-12, lists the two schools.
[41]M.I. Finley, *Economy and Society in Ancient Greece* (London, 1982), p. 125. Although Finley shows respect for Rostovtzeff's learning the frequency of his criticism suggests that Finley still considers him a dangerous foe methodologically even if "old-fashioned."

Alexander — an irreconcilable disagreement which can be judged only subjectively.

Nonetheless there is much still to be done on social and economic life, keeping in mind the vastness of the Hellenistic world, which was far from homogenous in economic levels. This work would best be undertaken from a specific stance as being a superb example of colonial imperialism. Everywhere the Greek and Macedonian successors of Alexander were political masters and tapped the riches of their subjects much as did the English, French, Dutch, and other exploiters of Asia and Africa until very recent times. Will in particular has written a superb essay comparing the Ptolemaic rule of Egypt with French imperialism in North Africa.[42]

Just as the English in India are often pictured — not always correctly — as reading aged copies of *The Times* over their gin slings at the Club, playing cricket, and disdaining the native babus, so the Greeks in the Near East appear fiercely wedded to their ancestral culture: "The Hellenistic world exhibits many of the traits of a colonial society, notably the conscious arrogance of cultural insecurity."[43] The idea that Alexander brought civilization to a region which had had millennia of settled cultural patterns is absurd, though it often lurks below the surface of modern Greek-oriented studies but it is true that in Hellenistic states Greek was the language of government, law, and literature. Only the Jews and then the Romans were able to resist this linguistic mastery which endured far down into the era of the Roman Empire. The military monarchs of the period were less tolerant of native ways than had been the Persian kings; so too Hellenic artistic models remained the base from which sculptors and other artists moved to create an urbane, if somewhat shallow style which was imitated from Carthage, Gaul, and Italy eastward to Bactria and India.

Although the reception of Hellenistic literature and art in the west must concern us in the next chapter, debate and varied views also abound on some fundamental characteristics of Hellenistic civiliza-

---

[42]E. Will, *The Craft of the Ancient Historian: Essays in Honor of Chester G. Starr* (Lanham, Maryland, 1985), pp. 273-301. See also from this point of view W.L. Westermann, *American Historical Review*, 43 (1937-8), pp. 271-87, and *Political Science Quarterly*, 40 (1925), pp. 517ff.; C. Preaux, *Atti* of the 11th International Papyrological Congress (Milan, 1966), pp. 475ff.

[43]Murray, *Journal of Roman Studies*, 67 (1977), p. 178, reviewing A. Momigliano, *Alien Wisdom: The Limits of Hellenization* (Cambridge, 1975), a valuable study. See also C. Habicht, *Vierteljahrschrift für Sozial-und Wirtschaftsgeschichte*, 45 (1958), pp. 5ff.

tion. Droysen, who began serious study of the age, talked of "fusion" of Greeks and Near Easterners; and the concept is far from dead – consider, for example, efforts to find Semitic influences in the thinking of Zeno of Citium or Posidonius of Apamea.[44] Again, the relation of Hellenistic concepts of monarchy and Iranian models is a "complex question, not always clear";[45] deification of rulers, variously practiced, has been widely explored as a precedent for late Roman and Byzantine styles of kingship. On the walls of the native temples of Egypt – and it must be recalled that the Ptolemies did as much construction of temples as any of the pharaohs – the rulers appear in ancestral poses, and their coronation ceremonies carried over some very ancient practices, including eventually crowning at Memphis.[46] Religiously the Greek inhabitants of Fayum villages were quite willing to worship the crocodile god as well as the Hellenic deities or their deified rulers; but the degree to which the deliberate creation of the cult of Sarapis was intended to unite Greeks and Egyptians is much debated.[47]

The evidence is thus two-sided, but in the main one may feel that "fusion" was very secondary to "diffusion."[48] Even if Alexandria and Antioch were, much as modern Hongkong or Bombay, inhabited largely by natives, the official patterns of government and public cults were Greek. The intruders sought earnestly to maintain their inheritance, especially via the education of the young in gymnasia, which flourished not only in cities but also in the Egyptian countryside.[49] One source of the dissensions in Jerusalem which produced the Maccabean upheaval was the creation of a gymnasium

[44]Cumont thought Posidonius was affected by his "Syrian" background, Reinhardt admitted a bit; Wilamowitz-Moellendorff and Bevan totally denied it. See recently M. Laffranque, *Poeidonios d'Apamée* (Paris, 1964).

[45]Will, *Le monde grec et l'Orient*, 2, p. 422.

[46]I. Noshy, *The Arts in Ptolemaic Egypt* (London, 1937).

[47]See Fraser, *Alexandria*, pp. 246-76; W. Hornbostel, *Sarapis* (Leiden, 1973; *Etudes preliminaires*, 32).

[48]Will, pp. 339ff., presents a balanced discussion; for the ambiguities in Jewish attitudes see M. Hadas, *Hellenistic Civilization* (New York, 1972), the subtitle of which is "Fusion and Diffusion."

[49]J. Delorme, *Gymnasion* (Paris, 1960), with the corrections in *Journal of Egyptian Archaeology*, 47 (1961), p. 144; Marrou, *History of Education*, Part II. W.L. Westermann drew a fascinating contrast between the cultural level of Zenon and a Mississippi overseer for James K. Polk, in *American Historical Review*, 47 (1941), pp. 64-72. In piety let me note the essay on Ptolemaic gymnasia by my first instructor in ancient history, T.A. Brady, in *University of Missouri Studies*, 11 (1936), pp. 9-20.

there and the tendency of young upperclass Jews to adopt Hellenic dress and custom; across the Hellenistic world Greek culture was so attractive that Hebrew often yielded to Greek, and in the synagogues (a Greek word itself) gentile artistic models were widely imitated.[50]

Not always, however, did either Jews or other natives accept Hellenism completely; Jewish religious leaders began, more especially from the second century after Christ onwards, the commentary on the Torah which led on to the Talmudic tradition, a deliberate turn away from Greek influences.[51] Though open revolt was rare, Egyptians and others could sabotage the system of exploitation and clutched to their heart visions of the overthrow of their masters.[52]

In ancient accounts of Hellenistic history, such as that of Polybius, the monarchs occupy the center of the stage; their power rested, as Lysimachus wrote to the inhabitants of Priene, "mostly on his own *arete*, also by reason of the good will of his friends and powers (*dynameis*)";[53] the latter, in turn, included the bureaucracy, the army, and the cities. The role of the urban centers in all aspects of Hellenistic life was vital, though the place of their citizens has not always been properly evaluated.

Except in Egypt the surplus of rural production largely flowed into the hands of urban landlords, the temples, or public coffers. Industrial production was centered in the cities, including the vigorous shops of Alexandria. Foreign trade in all commodities and products moved through the markets and harbors of the cities. An excellent study of economic growth in modern times draws the corollary. Unlike agriculture foreign trade "is almost always monetized . . . and it is physically channeled through a relatively small number of localities, making it relatively easy to mulct."[54] And of course it was the kings who needed to mulct to pay their

[50]E.R. Goodenough, *Jewish Symbols in the GrecoRoman Period*, 13 vols. (New York, 1953-68); more briefly, E.L. Sukenik, *Ancient Synagogues in Palestine and Greece* (London, 1934). The abundant literature is cited by Momigliano, *Alien Wisdom*; see also V. Tcherikover, *Hellenistic Civilization and the Jews* (New York, 1970); M. Hengel, *Judaism and Hellenism* (2d ed.; London, 1974).

[51]See the brief summary of the revisions in this matter by J. Neusner and others in W. Meeks, *The First Urban Christians* (New Haven, 1983), pp. 32-33.

[52]S.K. Eddy, *The King Is Dead* (Lincoln, Nebraska, 1961).

[53]Welles, *Royal Correspondence*, no. 6. "Modern literature on the Hellenistic state is as good as lacking," as Ehrenberg observes, though one might cite M. Hammond, *City-State and World State* (Cambridge, Mass., 1951), cc. 2-4, and Ehrenberg's own discussion in *The Greek State*.

[54]J.D. Gould, *Economic Growth in History* (London, 1972), pp. 218-19.

mercenaries and bureaucrats and keep up their expensive courts. The cities under Seleucid power often provided lump sums; the Ptolemies at times levied direct taxes on cities which they controlled.[55] If there were six Syrian wars, the aim in part was prestige, but there were also strong economic reasons in the desire to dominate the Syrian ports through which eastern wares, spices, and incense reached the Mediterranean. When Rome turned Delos into a free port the Senate knew very well what it was doing — delivering a devastating blow to the harbor tolls of Rhodes.

If the cities were milked, so too the kings in recompense had to support the local upper classes and more generally be generous with titles, honors, even contributions for civic purposes. Welles has been criticized for picturing the policy of the Seleucids toward their cities too idealistically; the reality is that the kings "might use sweet persuasion or the whip."[56] Ehrenberg concludes, after reviewing the tangled and contradictory evidence, that "the mutual relations of Polis and monarchy defy as a whole any legal definition or, in fact, any rationalization; they were entirely based on actual conditions of power."

Although Rostovtzeff went much too far in making the citizens bourgeois, their motives, as displayed in the plays of Menander, were selfish and materialistic, and men sought a quiet life. Yet the inhabitants of Ephesus, Priene, and other cities were in Nock's phrase "citizens, not subjects," and were very deeply attached to their communities, a fact often ignored or scanted. City-dwellers did not often venture far beyond their gates; outside political and cultural currents came to their notice largely through visitors such as royal representatives, artists, rhetoricians, and troupes of Dionysiac artists. Within their microcosms, however, the upper classes are visible in inscriptions as arranging endowments to pay for public teachers and doctors and contributing generously for aqueducts and other purposes. In particular they were honored by decrees for helping in times of food shortages; at Rhodes assistance to the food supply was a regular obligation or liturgy, and the closeknit oligarchy which controlled that state carefully saw to it that the lower orders were given necessary aid to keep them tractable.

"Hellenistic man" is often pictured as totally individualistic. A

[55]R.S. Bagnall, *The Administration of the Ptolemaic Possessions Outside Egypt* (Leiden, 1976).

[56]Ehrenberg, *Greek State*, pp. 191-94; W. Orth, *Königlicher Machtanspruch und städtische Freiheit* (Munich, 1977).

favorite adjective in modern treatments is uprooted; and the rise of the great Hellenistic philosophies, addressed to the uncertainties of life for an individual, along with the appearance of Near Eastern mystery religions, is adduced as proof of the lack of those social and political ties which had enfolded classical Greeks. In truth, however, the noted philosopher of the second century, Panaetius, adapted Stoic doctrines to encompass the responsibilities of a citizen, a stance intended not for his Roman friends but for his Rhodian compatriots;[57] we would do well to drop the concept of "deraciné" from discussions of the ordinary Hellenistic city-dweller. The great days of the Stoic and Epicurean doctrines were, I suspect, to come only in Roman times; certainly the mystery religions became most evident following the age of Caesar and Christ. After the Hellenistic dynasties had all disappeared, the cities of the Greek East continued to exist, though they barely survived the horrors of the Roman civil wars. They warrant thoughtful attention.

[57]M.E. Reesor, *Political Theory of the Old and Middle Stoa* (New York, 1951).

III

THE ROMAN REPUBLIC

When the historian turns from the urbane, complex Hellenistic world to the primitive countryside of early Italy, the intellectual shift is jarring, but the transition must be made — many Italian tribes contributed significantly to the origins of Rome whereas early Greek *poleis* emerged from local native roots.[1] Almost always in modern studies, to be sure, once Rome is on the scene those other peoples retreat to the corners of the stage, an unjustified dismissal inasmuch as the interactions of Rome with its neighbors had powerful political and cultural effects on Roman expansion.[2] Eventually the Romans spread a common veneer over all the peninsula, an impressive achievement; for as soon as the Roman Empire disappeared in Italy its population began to split apart politically. Not until A.D. 1870 was reunification achieved, and even today the average Italian feels most attached to his own *paese*.

In general surveys of Roman history the early peoples of Italy appear only briefly; Montelius and Peet fixed firmly a standard picture of a backward peninsula in which forces from the outside were the only factors producing changes.

Frank's textbook, standard for a generation, notes the prehistoric period primarily to introduce the Indo-Europeans, "tall, well-built, fair-haired" with "a marked capacity for analytical thought and for orderly government, as well as a distinct ability to assimilate and appreciate high artistic ideals."[3] One might hope that by now the Indo-European myth has been fully exploded both for Italy and for Greece, but its sway over Europe and North America was so long unquestioned that "it keeps creeping back into scholarly work, and

---

[1]The most important study of Republican history in the past generation is that of G. de Sanctis, *Storia dei Romani*, 4 vols. (Turin, 1907-23; 2d ed. in part, Florence, 1956-69), though it remained incomplete. T. Mommsen, *Römische Geschichte*, 3 vols. (Berlin, 1854-56; 8th ed., 1888-94; somewhat erratic translation, Chicago reprint, 1957), remains a work to be consulted; his views will be cited at various points in this chapter. J. Bleicken, *Geschichte der römischen Republik* (2d ed.; Munich, 1982), gives a full bibliography; its text is not to be trusted.

[2]See as partial exceptions, W.V. Harris, *Rome in Etruria and Umbria* (Oxford, 1971); E.T. Salmon, *Samnium and the Samnites* (Cambridge, 1967). The relations between Rome and the Greek cities of the south have scarcely been touched, and the wealth of recent archeological evidence for the early Latin communities demands a new synthesis.

[3]T. Frank, *History of Rome* (New York, 1923), p. 2.

even the new *Cambridge Ancient History* provides instances.''[4] In reality, wherever people of Indo-European speech appear as intruders in the ancient world it is as raping, burning, looting barbarians.

Vigorous archeological exploration, leading to syntheses by Peroni, Puglisi, Radmilli, and others, has dictated continuous elaboration and adjustment of the picture set by Montelius and Peet; one scholar has gone even further in seeking to demolish the conventional view completely. For Barker the early Italians were conservative, maintaining their traditions within many varieties of local culture, and these arose not from invasion or external influence but from native sources.[5] It is now clear that settlement on the site of Rome went back into the second millennium B.C., but as an organized state Rome emerged only in the eighth century—the period in which the Greek *poleis* were consolidated, though we always tend to picture Rome as chronologically retarded. So too, like the Greek upper classes, the leading elements in the Latin communities were acquiring luxuries, though they largely bought foreign goods rather than native products, as in Greece.

The vital problem for students of Roman history under the kings and in the earliest stage of the Republic is the degree to which the literary tradition, imbedded in Livy most fully, can be trusted: how could a writer in the time of Augustus know what happened six and seven centuries earlier?[6] For a time hypercriticism ruled; of late there has been a swing back toward acceptance of at least the main lines of the conventional story. The discovery of archaic altars and votive inscriptions at Lavinium, the evidence that Aeneas was revered there as Pater Indiges and was a popular figure among the Etruscans at least by the fifth century,[7] and above all archeological research in the Forum and other Roman sites bring physical support to many aspects of the literary story; by 600 Rome was a significant center in western Italy under Etruscan domination. To continue the parallel with Greek development, it may be recalled that the Agora in Athens

---

[4]E. Badian in *The Craft of the Ancient Historian* (Lanham, Maryland, 1985), p. 9.

[5]G. Barker, *Landscape and Society* (London, 1981); P. Peroni, *L'Età del bronzo nella peninsula italiana*, 1 (Florence, 1971); S.M. Puglisi, *La civiltà appennenica* (Florence, 1959); A.M. Radmilli, in *Popoli e civiltà dell'Italia antica*, 1 (Rome, 1974), ed. M. Pallottino et al.

[6]R.M. Ogilvie, *A Commentary on Livy Books 1-5* (Oxford, 1965); T.J. Luce, *Livy: The Composition of His History* (Princeton, 1977).

[7]F. Castagnoli, *Studi Romani*, (1982), pp. 1-15; G. Dury-Moyaers, *Enée et Lavinium* (Brussels, 1981); and studies by Alföldi, Bömer, Galinski, and others.

became the focus of a true urban settlement only at the same time as the Forum was paved. Etruscan influence, however, was not the only external impetus; Corinthian, Attic, and Laconian pottery was found under S. Omobono in the Forum Boarium to attest that Rome was in contact with the Greek world as well.[8]

If the main lines of distant memory can be accepted, does this entitle us to go on and breath the air of reality into the Roman kings, beginning with even Romulus?[9] Efforts have been made to prove that Servius Tullius did create the system of tribes and reorganized the army in centuries, and perhaps even built a first rampart around parts of the city;[10] but here a healthy dose of scepticism is warranted. Taken as a whole the volume of recent work on Rome in the Kingdom and the transition to the Republic is a saddening exhibition of largely fruitless labor. Theories are manufactured out of whole cloth to show the ingenuity of their creators in a manner reminiscent of the imaginative reconstructions of early Greek history on which I commented in an earlier chapter; to cite only one example Hanell sought to demonstrate that down to 450 the consuls were merely assistants to kings.[11] This approach does not advance our real knowledge; far more useful is the magnificent and sober catalogue of the magistrates of the Republic by Broughton.[12] Equally to be regretted are the disagreements about the nature of early Roman institutions which have produced scholarly duels almost overpassing the bounds of scholarly politeness, as in the running battle between Momigliano and Alföldi ended only by the latter's death.[13]

As far as the internal history of Rome in the Early and Mid-

---

[8]I must omit here any effort to discuss Etruscan origins and history; L.A. Foresti, *Tesi ipotesi e considerazioni sull' origine degli Etruschi* (Vienna, 1974), surveys the contrasting views of Piganiol, Pallottino, and others.

[9]Momigliano, however, indignantly rejected my inference that he believed in Romulus in *Journal of Roman Studies*, 53 (1963), p. 112 (my essay in *Historia*, 14 [1965], p. 272).

[10]R. Thomsen, *King Servius Tullius* (Copenhagen, 1980); J. Heurgon, *The Rise of Rome to 264 B.C.* (Berkeley, 1973), pp. 146-51, which otherwise is a useful survey of early Roman history.

[11]K. Hanell, *Das altrömische eponyme Amt* (Lund, 1946).

[12]T.R.S. Broughton, *The Magistrates of the Roman Republic*, 2 vols. (New York, 1952); supplement 1984.

[13]The vehemence of the polemic can be judged from A. Alföldi, *Römische Frühgeschichte* (Heidelberg, 1971); E. Gjerstad, *Early Rome*, 6 vols. (Lund, 1953-73); see also the less impassioned essays in *Les Origines de la république romaine* (*Entretiens Hardt*, 13, 1966).

Republic, down to the First Punic War, is concerned three principal theses have long been dominant. First, the Romans began as an agricultural population, densely settled in villages. In the Kingdom some commerce and industry did appear, but during the dismal years after the foundation of the Republic these elements vanished; especially following the wave of colonization in the Mid-Republic the Romans were decisively fixed as "primarily an agricultural people."[14] Secondly, Rome had a conservative, timocratic form of government under the control of the patricians, who fixed their sway at the inception of the Republic. But the great mass of the population, the plebeians, found upper-class domination exploitive and reacted in the famous "struggle of the orders," which resulted in the technical establishment of democracy by 287, i.e., the acceptance of plebiscites by the plebeian assembly as having the force of law. And finally these developments took place within an almost closed society. In particular the Romans failed to be aware of the great days of classic Greece, and Greek influences remained marginal down to the beginning of the third century.[15]

These theses have come under attack, and at the least nuances and qualifications must be drawn.[16] No doubt most Romans were farmers – throughout ancient times inhabitation of all Mediterranean areas was primarily agricultural, for surpluses were too scanty to permit the urban tilt which we now take as natural. Latin and then Roman efforts to promote colonization also favored rural nuclei, as a way of binding the Italian peninsula together.[17] Yet we must not be misled by the eulogy of rural virtues so pronounced in Livy, Cicero, and other Latin writers. By 300 the city of Rome was one of the larger urban centers in the Mediterranean and so had to have seaborne wheat, and at that time – before overseas conquests – had to pay for its grain. Polished metal objects such as the Ficorini cista were

---

[14]Frank, *History of Rome*, p. 80; so too H. Last, *Cambridge Ancient History*, 7 (1928), c. xiv.

[15]All over the western Mediterranean (save at Spina) Greek evidence becomes much reduced in the fifth century, as I noted in chapter 1; the fact is observed for each local area but not placed in a general context for explanation.

[16]In following paragraphs I have drawn on my *Beginnings of Imperial Rome* (Ann Arbor, 1980).

[17]E.T. Salmon, *Roman Colonization under the Republic* (Ithaca, 1969); A. Giardina and A. Schiavone, eds., *Società romana e produzione schiavista*, 3 vols. (Rome/Bari, 1981), surveys from a Marxist point of view agricultural changes in both Republic and Early Empire.

made by Roman smiths; the products of the potters were exported to Sicily, north Africa, and the coasts of Gaul and Spain. These were areas open to Roman traders by treaties with Carthage; it may not be entirely proper to judge that Carthage alone set the terms of the agreements. The date at which Roman coinage began has been a source of contention, but the latest hoard evidence points clearly to its inception just before 300 – a date which is earlier than the first Carthaginian issues.[18]

So too Roman commerce by sea is quite visible once one discards conventional blinkers; it would be unwise to assume that governing circles in the Senate and elsewhere were totally oblivious to economic factors. Several scholars have demonstrated that in the later fourth century Roman upper classes were split between a Fabian faction favoring rural expansion and another group led by Q. Publilius Philo and then Appius Claudius which sought Greek connections and encouraged the growth of the urban population; the reforms and building energy of Appius Claudius as censor in 312 illuminate this latter policy. Incidentally the usual view of Roman aristocrats in this era as grave, bearded servants of the state without personal ambition is scarcely supported by the self-assertion of Appius Claudius, who impressed his name forever on the Roman landscape in naming a road, an aqueduct, and the rural market center of Forum Appii.[19]

Many aspects of the "struggle of the orders," such as the emphasis on debts, have long been suspect as reflecting discontent in the Late Republic, but recent work has gone much further in casting doubt on the standard picture of the nature of the two orders and their emergence in early Rome. Mitchell, indeed, would define the patrician class in terms reminiscent of Bourriot's treatment of the purported *gene* in Greek history.[20] Here, parenthetically, I may raise a query on one aspect which has always troubled me, though it never seems to receive attention: how could a lower class secure sufficient cohesion and independence of its superiors to create the famous

---

[18]*Coin Hoards*, 7 (1985), pp. 52-53; this date is supported by R. Mitchell and A. Burnett, and M.H. Crawford has come to accept it; in *Roman Republican Coinage*, 2 vols. (Cambridge, 1975), he had placed the earliest issues about 280.

[19]F. Cassola, *I gruppi politici romani nel III secolo a.C.* (Trieste, 1962); E.S. Staveley, *Historia*, 8 (1959), pp. 410-33.

[20]R. Mitchell in *The Conflict of Orders in Archaic Rome*, ed. K. Raaflaub (Berkeley, 1986); see also J.-C. Richard, *Les Origines de la Plebe romaine* (Paris, 1978), a 600-page dissertation with exhaustive presentation of modern views on every aspect of early Rome.

machinery of popular action, including assembly, officials and even treasury? This achievement, though "a wretched compromise" in Mommsen's eyes, is almost without parallel in other class-structured societies.

Finally, the matter of Greek influence. Down past the fall of the kings the import of Greek vases is well attested, then the number of fragments diminishes rapidly across the fifth century in testimony to Roman impoverishment, but pots are not necessarily the whole story. There is no reason to doubt the report that Rome dedicated a trophy at Delphi to commemorate its victory over Veii; visitors from Massilia were given a special viewing stand at Roman festivals; aristocrats such as Q. Publilius Philo and P. Sempronius Sophus had Greek cognomina, the latter received during the lifetime of Sempronius and proudly passed on to his heirs. More generally a recent colloquium has explored pervasive Hellenic influences throughout central Italy in the fourth century, and a magnificent exhibition was assembled a few years ago on material from Esquiline graves, Minerva Medica, and the Tiber to demonstrate that Roman figurine-makers and other artists were fully cognizant of Hellenistic styles at the time.[21] Bianchi Bandinelli adequately disproved the imputation that Rome at this time could not have supported artistic activity of any quality.[22] The major reason for general depreciation of Roman culture down past 300 is the fact that Livius Andronicus is considered to have begun the creation of Latin literature only in the mid-third century – historians still are influenced too much by the framework of classical philology – but even in this regard one must remember that Appius Claudius was the author of *Sententiae*, praised by Panaetius, and delivered a famous speech which Cicero knew.

Thus far we have concentrated on internal developments; abroad there was equally significant change in the expansion of Roman rule over all the peninsula as far as the Apennines and then overseas empire in Spain, Sardinia and Corsica, and Sicily in connection with the Punic wars.[23] To the Romans this growth of power was an inevitable consequence of their due observance of religious rites; as Cicero put it, "We have overcome all the nations of the world,

---

[21]*Hellenismus in Mittelitalien*, ed. P. Zanker (Göttingen, 1976); F. Coarelli ed., *Roma medio repubblicana* (Rome, 1973).

[22]In his essay in *Scritti in onore de Bartolomeo Nogara* (Vatican, 1937), pp. 11-20.

[23]A. Afzelius, *Die römische Eroberung Italiens (340-254 v. Chr.)* (Copenhagen, 1942); R.M. Errington, *The Dawn of Empire* (Ithaca, 1972), a factual narrative of expansion 264-133.

because we have realized that the world is directed and governed by the gods."[24] To survey views of Roman religious belief would, I must note, take us too far afield, but at least it may be observed that the cold, formalistic structure presented by Wissowa and others early in the century has largely yielded to a more sensitive portrayal of the irrational, even mystical, side of Roman beliefs.[25]

A recent work has argued that Hannibal's invasion of Italy represented the last opportunity for the peoples of the Mediterranean to remain independent of Roman rule and to maintain "all possibilities of free cultural development" and that it would have been far better for them if Hannibal had achieved his dream of breaking up the Roman confederacy.[26] When events are put in this light, perhaps we might think again – not about the unhappy aspects of conquest and Republican misrule, but about the eventual results of the Roman unification of the western Mediterranean. Would the Celtic peoples of Gaul and Spain have gone on to produce a plurality of cultures with great potential for the future of western Europe? Is there any valid reason for thinking that if Carthage, ruthless in exploiting its subjects, had become the major power the consequences would have been happier than those of Roman mastery?[27]

Those who suffered the brutality and rapine of Roman conquest might well judge matters differently at the time; in the previous chapter the question as to the degree to which Rome ruined the Hellenistic world was briefly noted. Plutarch wrote essays discussing whether Roman mastery reflected the victory of Fate or of Chance (Tyche), and a considerable body of anti-Roman propaganda appeared in the later years of the Republic.[28] The major turning point in Roman expansion after the conquest of Sicily was the Second

[24]*On the Responses of the Haruspices* 9.

[25]H. Wagenvoort, *Roman Dynamism* (Oxford, 1947); G. Dumezil, *Archaic Roman Religion*, 2 vols. (Chicago, 1970), whose theory of three Indo-European sectors is more useful here than in considering political organization. *Numen*, a concept much used in anthropological studies, does not actually appear in Latin until the late Republic (S. Weinstock, *Journal of Roman Studies*, 39 [1949], pp. 166-67).

[26]F.K. Kienitz, *Völker im Schatten* (Munich, 1981), p. 321.

[27]B.H. Warmington, *Carthage* (London, 1960), is the best account of Carthaginian history; problems connected with Phoenician colonization were noted in chap. 1.

[28]P. Jones, *Plutarch and Rome* (Oxford, 1971); Plutarch, *Moralia* 316ff.; J. Deininger, *Der politische Widerstand gegen Rom im Griechenland, 217-86 v. Chr.* (Berlin, 1971); A. Fuks, *Journal of Hellenic Studies*, 90 (1970), pp. 78-89 (now in *Social Conflict in Ancient Greece*, ed. M. Stern and M. Amit [Jerusalem-Leiden, 1984]; E. Gruen, *Journal of Hellenic Studies*, 96 (1976), pp. 46-69; J. Briscoe, *Past and Present*, 36 (1967), pp. 3-20.

Macedonian War, an event for which modern explanations have undergone a remarkable change. The standard view until very recently was that created by Mommsen, Frank, and especially Holleaux; these scholars drew a dramatic picture of noble Romans deeply attached to Greek culture, who suddenly reversed their policy of disinterest in Hellenistic politics, yielded to the wily persuasion of Rhodian and Pergamene ambassadors, and declared war on Philip V with the genuine intent of liberating Greece.

This idealistic interpretation of "sentimental politics" has been much debated and criticized in many of its details; Badian, for example, has pointed out that if we turn to the annalistic tradition Rome did not totally withdraw from Greek matters after the end of the First Macedonian War in 205.[29] Stier still believes in Roman philhellenism, but few others concur; Gruen thus rightly distinguishes between admiration for Greek culture and Roman political activity: "The very idea of philhellenism as national policy would be unintelligible to a Roman."[30] Recently Harris has simply cut the Gordian knot in a sweeping study; Rome deliberately and continuously engaged in expansion from the late fourth century onward, its aristocracy seeking repute in an "ideology of *laus* and *gloria*" and secondarily acquiring economic profit from the fruits of victory. In the latter point Harris gains support from the exploration by Hopkins of the rise of slavery in Italy.[31] Possibly Harris puts Roman policies in a too systematic and intellectual light; accidents and mistakes do affect the foreign policy of any state, but in general a fragment of Polybius presents much the same view: "The Romans took no ordinary forethought not to appear to be the initiators of unjust actions and not to appear to be attacking those around them when they took on wars, but always to seem to be acting in self-defense and

---

[29]E. Badian, *Foreign Clientelae (264-70 B.C.)* (Oxford, 1958), pp. 61-63; J.P.V.D. Balsdon, *Journal of Roman Studies*, 44 (1954), pp. 30-42.

[30]H.E. Stier, *Roms Aufstieg zur Weltmacht und die griechische Welt* (Köln/Opladen, 1957); Gruen, *Hellenistic Monarchies*, p. 271; After convassing the many explanations offered for the outbreak of the Second Macedonian War he settles (p. 397) on senatorial pride. See also G. Brizzi, *I sistemi informatici dei Romani* (Wiesbaden, 1962), pp. 51-61, on other modern views.

[31]W.V. Harris, *War and Imperialism in Republican Rome, 327-70 B.C.* (Oxford, 1978), pp. 30ff.; K. Hopkins, *Conquerors and Slaves* (Cambridge, 1978), c. 1: E. Badian, *Roman Imperialism in the Late Republic* (2d ed.; Oxford, 1968), discounts economic factors, especially as presented in Marxist terms. See the papers in *The Imperialism of Mid-Republican Rome* (Papers and Monographs 29, American Academy in Rome, 1984).

to enter upon wars out of necessity.''[32]

It is quite evident from a widening range of sources that the senatorial aristocracy or *nobilitas* arrogated to itself an ever more prominent position from the early second century onward. In a closely reasoned essay Millar has shown that Polybius' portrayal of a mixed constitution in his era did have justification inasmuch as the assemblies still at that time had some role,[33] but thereafter senatorial domination of the organs of government was unquestioned until the upheavals incited by the Gracchi brothers. Since Münzer paved the way, recent treatments of the internal politics of Rome have been cast far too much in terms of factions which are analyzed by prosopographical methods;[34] but the popularity of chasing down who was whose uncle may at last be waning.[35] Biographies of leaders such as Scipio Aemilianus, for whom we now have sufficient data, are not cast in such narrow terms.[36] More useful have been studies of concepts such as *clientela, otium*, and other factors shaping Roman life outside the purely legal structure, yet one must in treating Roman history always keep an eye on its legal framework, though this ''is a jungle into which visitors stray at the risk of getting lost or in fear of being mauled by the resident scholarly tigers.''[37]

By the second century Roman aristocrats also became ostentatious and were far more at home in Hellenistic culture, including an interest in its philosophic schools; the famous opposition to the debilitating effects of Greek civilization led by Cato the Elder was only partial and superficial. We must, however, not construe the advance of eastern ways in Rome purely in intellectual terms. Cato's

---

[32]Polybius fr. 99, quoted by P.S. Derow, *Journal of Roman Studies*, 69 (1979), pp. 1-15.

[33]*Journal of Roman Studies*, 74 (1984), pp. 1-19; here one may note also the valuable studies by L.R. Taylor, *The Voting Districts of the Roman Republic* (Rome, 1960) and *Roman Voting Assemblies* (Ann Arbor, 1966).

[34]F. Münzer, *Römische Adelsparteien und Adelsfamilien* (Stuttgart, 1920; 2d ed., 1963); M. Gelzer, *The Roman Nobility* (New York, 1969); H.H. Scullard, *Roman Politics 220-156 B.C.* (2d ed.; Oxford, 1973), defends the prosopographical approach in his preface.

[35]In a detailed study, *Der Einfluss des Wahlleiters bei den römischen Consulwahlen von 361 bis 50 v. Chr.* (Munich, 1976), R. Rilinger demolishes one foundation of prosopographical theory by showing that consuls did not entirely control who was elected as their successors. Monographs can at times have general utility.

[36]A.E. Astin, *Scipio Aemilianus* (Oxford, 1967), and *Cato the Censor* (Oxford, 1978).

[37]Hopkins, *Conquerors and Slaves*, p. 80, who gives some basic bibliography, through omitting the major works of A. Watson; see also E. Meyer, *Römischer Staat und Staatsgedanke* (3d ed.; Zurich, 1964).

model might be Manius Curius, who boiled his own turnips in a hut; but Plutarch slyly notices that Cato in his later years could stride, whip in hand, to his kitchen to rebuke poor service or improper preparation of his dinner. The schools of massage in Alexandria trained specialists to relax Roman aristocrats,[38] and social vices such as divorce, childlessness, and even family murder began to appear in the upper classes:

Thus right and wrong became confused; mankind in darkness,
bewildered now ignored the gods.
Never again do gods return to earth or walk with men
in the bright sun of noon.[39]

To support their elegant life style aristocrats had to have money, which they gained in part from booty and the perquisites of office in the provinces; behind the scenes they also served as guarantors for tax-collectors and as money-lenders. The rapacity of Verres and the ruthless use of public influence by Brutus to collect his 48% interest from the hapless councillors of Soli are well known, but it has been shown in several recent studies that the equestrians did not always operate as a distinct class to influence state policy, as suggested by Hill in a book with a misleading title.[40] On the other hand, the activities of the two nobles just named demonstrate that we must not go too far in denying to the leaders of the Roman world any economic interest; maintenance of luxury in a competitive age called for wealth on a scale unprecedented in earlier history, or at least the ability to run up debts on the degree which Caesar attained during his rise.[41]

As far as the provincials were concerned, Roman misgovernment was more noticeable in the fact that governors changed every year and were rarely conversant with or interested in local problems beyond trying to keep their province peaceful. Equally offensive was the conscious or unconscious arrogance of Romans in the east, all too often like "the ugly American" in contemptuous disregard for ancestral customs and pride. This topic, including the hamstringing

[38]M.I. Finley, *Ancient Slavery and Modern Ideology* (London, 1980), p. 106, who notes Pliny the Younger used an Egyptian freedman for massage.

[39]Catullus 64 (tr. Gregory).

[40]H. Hill, *The Roman Middle Class* (Oxford, 1952); P.A. Brunt, *Trade and Politics in the Ancient World.* 1 (Paris, 1965), pp. 118-37; C. Nicolet, *L'Ordre équestre à l'époque républicaine*, 2 vols. (Paris, 1966-74); E. Badian, *Publicans and Sinners* (Oxford, 1972).

[41]I. Shatzman, *Senatorial Wealth and Roman Politics* (Brussels, 1975); A. Ferrill, *Ancient World*, 1 (1975), pp 169-77. On the interest of senators in gain see E. Gruen, *Papers and Monographs of the American Academy in Rome*, 29 (1984), p. 68.

of elephants in the zoo at Antioch, Scipio Aemilianus forcing the corpulent Ptolemy Physcon to waddle to the harbor to greet him, or the murder of a cat by a Roman in Alexandria, deserves thoughtful study, for its consequences were far-reaching.[42]

In 88, that is to say, the Greek east was led by Mithridates Eupator in a great insurrection against Roman rule, which drew in even the somnolent university town of Athens. All too often this revolt is treated briefly as a minor aspect of the career of Sulla, but it warrants careful exploration for its own sake, especially to explain why eventually the leaders of the Greek cities abandoned Mithridates and swung back to the Roman side.[43] This adherence was not shattered by the exactions and devastion of the Roman civil wars in the next generation, but continued to be a powerful force on down across the centuries of the Empire; indeed the long survival of the Byzantive state rested ultimately on decisions taken in the time of Mithridates.

The last generation of the Roman Republic is always portrayed in somber tones as an era of the dissolution of public order and contending generals, yet Rome added in this period more territory to its empire than in any preceding short age and nourished a varied literary outburst in the figures of Caesar, Cicero, Catullus, Lucretius, Sallust, Varro and others. Our evidence now extends to include works by major actors such as Caesar and Cicero – though not Pompey, who remains a puzzle despite three recent biographies; Cicero too continues to be a diversely judged figure in his political role even if few would go so far in depreciation as did Carcopino. No one, however, could disagree with Caesar's judgment that "he advanced the boundaries of the Latin genius."[44]

As our information mounts so too does the complexity of events, well narrated by Gruen in a recent study.[45] Efforts to explain the motive forces usually extend back no farther than the Gracchi, who

---

[42]An amusing bit of evidence on the concern of Hellenistic bureaucrats to satisfy visiting Romans is the Egyptian order of 112 B.C. to make sure that tidbits for the crocodiles were laid on and "in general take the greatest pains in everything to see that the visitor is satisfied" (*Select Papyri*, ed. A.S. Hunt and C.C. Edgar, 2 [London, 1934], no. 416 P. Tebtunis 33)

[43]See especially D. Magie, *Roman Rule in Asia Minor*, 2 vols. (Princeton, 1950).

[44]Pliny, *Natural History* 2. 91; J Carcopino, *Cicero: The Secrets of His Correspondence* (London, 1951). Carcopino was a fascinating scholar, acute in specific comments but virtually always wrong-headed in major theses.

[45]E.S. Gruen, *The Last Generation of the Roman Republic* (Berkeley, 1974).

have been harshly judged from Mommsen onward;[46] this approach is too narrowly political. As Toynbee emphasized in a rather unsatisfactory but lengthy study, the character of Italian social and economic life had been in revolution since the third century;[47] one must keep in mind also the rise of commerce and industry in the cities of the peninsula, well described by Rostovtzeff. The product was the consolidation of self-reliant upper classes who eventually secured citizenship in the Social War and provided a vital element in the eventual success of Augustus – but that is running ahead of our story.[48]

When one plunges into the welter of modern studies on the late Republic it appears that nothing really new can be said in detail, but then one comes on the brilliant article by Badian analyzing the situation in Rome before Sulla's return or Meier's dense but thoughtful work on the role of the aristocracy, bound by personal ties, and the ''Extensivierung'' of the body politic as equestrians, urban proletariat, and army became more important players on the stage.[49] Meier in particular rejects the recent Russian effort to interpret the declining Republic as an era mainly of social upheaval; but a police force was impossible within the senatorial regime.

Since I am not a specialist in this complex period I cannot make specific suggestions of areas which would repay further investigation, but I may note that I have never understood why discussions of the wellsprings of change are always couched in terms of the senatorial and equestrian orders, an infinitesimal proportion of the population of Rome, which may have run to half a million.[50] It is worth noting that the first extraordinary command, which paved the way for

[46]See R.E. Smith, *The Failure of the Roman Republic* (New York, 1976); on the Gracchi most recently D. Stockton, *The Gracchi* (Oxford, 1979)

[47]A. Toynbee, *Hannibal's Legacy*, 2 vols. (Oxford, 1965).

[48]A.N. Sherwin-White, *The Roman Citizenship* (2d ed.; Oxford, 1973), discusses the views of Badian, Brunt, Gabba, and Salmon; more on this explosion might be derived from the coinage of the federates.

[49]E. Badian, *Journal of Roman Studies*, 52 (1962), pp. 47-61; C. Meier, *Res publica amissa* (Wiesbaden, 1966).

[50] This is the estimate of P.A. Brunt, *Italian Manpower 225 B.C.-A.D. 14* (Oxford, 1971), an exemplary work in its caution. Hopkins, *Conquors and Slaves*, pp. 96-98, opts for a figure closer to a million – too high in my judgment. On violence see J. Heaton, *Mob Violence in Late Roman Republic 133-49 B.C.* (reprint Ann Arbor, 1968); A.W. Lintott, *Violence in Republican Rome* (Oxford, 1968); P.A. Brunt, *Past and Present*, 35 (1966), pp. 3ff. More generally, C. Nicolet, *Le Métier de citoyen dans la Rome républicaine* (Paris, 1976).

Caesar's sweeping power in Gaul, was given to Pompey to cope with the uncertainties of Roman food supplies.[51] The populace may not have had a direct role, except in riots and gang warfare, but its hidden pressures must be taken into account in discussing both Caesar and Augustus.

And so to Caesar, who has bewitched later generations more than any other ancient secular figure; modern work on his career is voluminous enough to demand a whole book of bibliography.[52] The most thoughtful essays in recent literature are Strasburger's discussions of his almost accidental early career and then of his bitter last years;[53] Caesar ended the Republic but never could he have succeeded, as Augustus did, in establishing a viable, lasting new form of government. Kraft has brilliantly established from numismatic evidence the fact that Caesar principally wished to be visualized as inheriting Etruscan royal paraphernalia — a severe blow to the common idea that Caesar sought to be a monarch of Hellenistic type.[54] Explanation of the forces which drove him, however, will always be debated; Mommsen put his finger closest to the truth in observing that the very rationality which marked Caesar perhaps more than any other politician in all history was at once his strength and his undoing, as he lay dead, without bodyguard, at the foot of the statue of Pompey. When Plutarch came to write a biography of Caesar he simply described his career, the only figure in all his work for whom he felt an inadequacy to pass judgment. Shakespeare deserves the last word (in the mouth of Cassius):

Why, man, he doth bestride the narrow world
Like a Colossus; and we petty men
Walk about under his huge legs, and peep about
To find ourselves dishonourable graves.

[51]This was suggested by Brunt at a conference of German and English scholars in London at which I, as an outsider, raised the query given in the text; see more fully his *Social Conflicts in the Roman Republic* (London, 1971).

[52]H. Gesche, *Caesar* (Darmstadt, 1976), a list of over 1900 books and articles; the most recent addition is C. Meier, *Caesar* (Berlin, 1982), a best seller in Germany.

[53]H. Strasburger, *Studien zur Alten Geschichte*, 1, pp. 181-327, 343-421.

[54]K. Kraft, *Jahrbuch für Numismatik und Geldgeschichte*, 3/4 (1952-53). pp. 7-97; H. Volkmann, *Das Staatsdenken der Römer* (Darmstadt, 1966).

IV

THE ROMAN EMPIRE

Three great authors tower in the advancement of our understanding of the Roman Empire. The most influential study was not written yesterday; indeed its first volume was published in the famous year of 1776. Edward Gibbon's masterpiece is thus the oldest work which one can still read with profit in ancient history, though it also has considerable interest as a reflection of the intellectual attitudes of its era. As has recently been observed, Gibbon's mind was marked by "flexible sympathies, open-mindedness and, above all, passion for truth."[1]

Next must come Mommsen's voluminous output. Some of the 1200-odd products of his pen considered the Republic, including the great synthesis for which he was the second author to receive the Nobel Prize, but the majority of his essays and books related to the Empire. Unfortunately he never wrote the fourth volume of his *Römische Geschichte*, which would have given us a general appreciation of imperial history; even had he done so, one must doubt that the work would have adequately countered a fundamental weakness in our views of the Empire, an issue to which I shall return shortly. Mommsen may be criticized as discussing history largely in institutional, legalistic terms; few of us nowadays would accept his argument that the Augustan system was a true partnership between *princeps* and Senate, a dyarchy, though if he had spoken in terms of the senatorial aristocracy as a social class it would be more difficult to disagree.[2] Nonetheless he remains a historian usually cited with respect and still often imitated;[3] my first book, on the Roman imperial navy, was cast largely in Mommsenian terms as an account of an institution based largely on inscriptions.

Third is Syme, who established his reputation with a remarkable study of the men and factors which attended Augustus' rise to power; thereafter he has continued to pour out articles and books, the latter

---

[1] P.R. Ghosh, *Journal of Roman Studies*, 73 (1983), pp. 1-23, at p. 20.

[2] M. Hammond, *The Augustan Principate* (enl. ed. New York, 1968), is among the few still accepting Mommsen; in *The Roman Empire: A Study in Survival* (New York, 1982), I distinguished between the Senate, a useful sounding board, and the senatorial aristocracy, powerful in many areas of life.

[3] Thus D. Musti, *Gnomon*, 54 (1982), pp. 298-300, finds in K. Christ, *Römische Geschichte*, (Darmstadt, 1973), a Mommsenian approach.

especially on Latin historians.[4] Syme's mastery of the sources and total recall of a wealth of modern literature are phenomenal, but in two respects his influence has been deleterious. While he himself wrote in a clipped, epigrammatic style reminiscent of Tacitus, those who have tried to copy him have not always been so successful. Again, his emphasis on the prosopographical approach has been far too widely taken up by lesser lights, who cannot extract the significance of family times which he often uncovers. In this respect I may note that one of my former students once ventured to query Sir Ronald on whether Namier's similar approach to eighteenth-century parliaments had influenced him; the reply was that he had not heard of Namier's work when writing his own study – but Münzer and Gelzer were sufficient models for anyone concerned with Roman history.[5]

Further conceptual progress has not been notable; if anything we have retrogressed. Earlier I quoted Momigliano's view that Greek history was in a state of crisis; the truth is that if any era of ancient history is in disarray and uncertainty it is the Early Roman Empire. The trouble is not lack of attention; by far the largest volume of scholarly effort is devoted to the Empire, with its wealth of every type of source. The many volumes parading as a Festschrift for Vogt are impressive testimony to this wide range of investigation; yet if one pulls down these fat volumes in their orange dust jackets and reads extensively one comes to feel that in basic concepts much is amiss.[6] We have lost that sureness of outlook and confidence of approach which marked the work of Gibbon, Mommsen, Syme, and also Rostovtzeff.

For the jubilee volume of the *Journal of Roman Studies* I was asked to survey work on the Roman Empire 1911-60, an interesting challenge which sometimes led me to unexpected conclusions. One, not altogether surprising, was the proliferation of tongues; whereas items in seven languages appeared in the first volume of *L'Année Philologique* (1924-26), by 1957 13 languages could have been useful, though I think Syme went too far in criticizing in a review an author who failed to read an article in Serbo-Croatian.

More amazing was the steady decline in German scholarship after

---

[4]E. Badian and A.R.Birley have edited his *Roman Papers*, 3 vols. (Oxford, 1979-84).
[5]A. Ferrill (personal communication). Parenthetically Peel could still burst out in 1835, "Damn the Whigs, they are all cousins."
[6]*Aufstieg und Niedergang der römischen Welt*, ed. H. Temporini (Berlin, 1972-).

the First World War; in 1924-26 44% of the total was in German, but thirty years later German titles were only 17%, well below English (30%, more used by European scholars these days) and Italian (26%). The rise of Italian attention to Roman history has continued and has since produced the massive study of constitutional history by de Martino, thoughtful essays by Gabba, the extraordinary range of Mazzarino's studies, and other worthy successors to de Sanctis and Fraccaro.

Equally noticeable has been the preference for cultural, as against political history, a tendency which has merits and also defects in some of its assumptions; for example, were classical men completely rational, and especially in their Roman phase were they simply imitators of Greek models? In the end I reached the conclusion that "above all we desperately need a political history of the Roman Empire, which is solid and well-buttressed . . . the product of a single individual's pen and masterful vision," and more prophetically than I was then aware ended the survey with the query, "Can progress on the detailed level take place if general conceptual schemes are absent, or are merely a dead inheritance from past thought?"[7] That in a nutshell is the problem today.

Down into the 1920's detailed studies such as Mommsen's survey of the provinces and Rostovtzeff's heavily documented social and economic history supported a generally favorable view of the Early Empire as an era in which the "Roman peace" was consolidated, prosperity abounded, and orderly government prevailed. This approach dominated a host of more general appreciations such as those of Mattingly and Nilsson and provoked little serious dissent. Since then our attitudes have changed markedly to open hostility at times; the word "peace" often is coupled with the biting statement in Tacitus, "They make a desert and call it peace."[8] In part this alteration reflects the growing unease of intellectuals in the political turmoil of contemporary decades, but it certainly can be justified in our sources. For the Roman Republic no such shift has been necessary; even an apologist for Rome such as Frank, who could lay the responsibility for the Second Punic War on the perfidious Hannibal, had to admit some black pages into his account — as the

[7] *Journal of Roman Studies*, 50 (1960), pp. 149-60 (now in *Essays on Ancient History*, pp. 301-12).

[8] *Agricola* 30; note that the phrase was not even verbally original with Tacitus (Pliny, *Natural History* 6. 182). See my survey of the change in *Aufstieg und Niedergang*, 1 pp. 3-11 = *Essays on Ancient History*, pp. 213-21).

unwarranted seizure of Sardinia and Corsica — and others had always admitted the brutality of Roman conquest and Republican misgovernment. But the steady onmarch of Roman expansion and the companion cultural progress of the Romans could be put on the balance scales as compensating factors.

Not so for the Early Empire: if it were not a noble structure in the first two centuries after Christ, the historian could only look forward to the horror to come in the chaos of the third century and the absolutism of the Late Empire. Yet if many of us cannot cast our detailed studies against a harmonious, optimistic background, no other has been systematically advanced in recent literature, i.e., there is no general treatment of the Early Empire in continuously critical terms — perhaps it would be impossible to write such a work, though at least in American history such hostile surveys have been produced by William Appleman Williams and others. So we flounder, often unconsciously, and bury ourselves in facts without seeking their general application.

The wealth of special studies on individual emperors, on the growth of organs of the imperial bureaucracy, on particular provinces and even cities can be assessed through essays in the Vogt series and in three recent surveys with good bibliographies.[9] Here I would single out two: Hopkins' careful exploration of the senatorial aristocracy, especially in regard to the failure of sons to succeed their senatorial fathers, and Millar's broadly based assessment of the role of the emperor, one of the widest panoramas in recent work even though Millar makes the *princeps* too passive, reacting to petitions, and does not adequately consider his military role.[10] After all, one who would be emperor had to have the support of the army, the senatorial aristocracy, and the bureaucracy; and loss of any one of the three — usually all of them — brought a sudden end to a reign.

The ancient historians of the Empire sat usually in Rome, not on the throne of the Caesars but at the dinner tables of rumor-mongering aristocrats; events in the provinces and on the frontiers received notice only when there was insurrection or foreign war. We

---

[9]A Garzetti, *From Tiberius to the Antonines* (London, 1974); P. Petit, *Pax Romana* (Berkeley, 1976); F. Millar and others, *The Roman Empire and its Neighbours* (London, 1967).

[10]Hopkins and G. Burton, *Death and Renewal* (Cambridge, 1983), c. 3; F. Millar, *The Emperor in the Roman World* (London, 1977). My judgment of the latter work is not altogether that of Hopkins in *Journal of Roman Studies*, 68 (1978), pp. 178-86.

cannot follow them in this limitation;[11] in particular one must always keep one's eye on the cities, especially those of the Greek East, which grew steadily in economic and cultural strength during the first two centuries after Christ. The frontiers also deserve attention as a membrane enclosing the living tissue of city and countryside; only so long as the army and navy controlled passage across the boundaries was the Empire safe. In recent years there has been much more consideration of the frontiers, encompassing periodic congresses of frontier studies, and a modern strategic analyst has essayed to survey the shifts in frontier policy. Although Luttwak makes matters too systematic, his discussion is well-based and along proper lines.[12] Study of the Roman army has also gone beyond earlier works which simply catalogued legions, auxilia, and weapons to more careful analysis of recruitment, which has its surprise, and the life of the soldiers; but I do not think we have exhausted military topics.[13]

The strength of the army rested on the prosperity and internal stability of the Early Empire. The former is well illustrated in the remains of its cities, rural villas, and an abundance of artistic and utilitarian objects from Britain to Syria and North Africa. In a famous study Rostovtzeff described this burgeoning world, though he is nowadays severely criticized for his optimism and bourgeois prejudices, as I noted in regard to his massive Hellenistic work. The landscape of the Empire was not as tranquil as he suggested; rural brigandage, revolts of the Jews, and other upheavals did occur.[14] Yet

[11]Millar, *Journal of Roman Studies*, 56 (1966), p. 166, urges that we look from the provinces toward the center; so too C. Nicolet, *Rome et la conquête du monde méditerranéen*, 2 (Paris, 1978).

[12]E.N. Luttwak, *The Grand Strategy of the Roman Empire from the First Century A.D. to the Third* (Baltimore, 1976); S.L. Dyson, *The Creation of the Roman Frontier*, (Princeton, 1985), finds the origins of imperial policy in the Republic.

[13]On recruitment see especially J.C. Mann, *Hermes*, 91 (1963), pp. 483-89; and G. Forni, *Il Reclutamento delle legioni da Augusto a Diocleziano* (Milan, 1953), and in *Aufstieg und Niedergang*, 2. 1, pp. 339-91. My colleague Eadie has recently remarked of M. Speidel, *Roman Army Studies*, 1 (Amsterdam, 1984), that it "defines the main directions of research on the Roman military during the past decade more clearly than recent studies of imperialism and grand strategy." (*American Historical Review*, 90 [1985], p. 1171).

[14]R. MacMullen, *Enemies of the Roman Order* (Cambridge, Mass., 1967); L. Mildenberg, *The Coinage of the Bar Kokhba War* (Aarau, 1984), goes beyond a thorough catalogue to illuminate this revolt as a whole. On the general history of the Jews in the Roman Empire one must certainly note the thorough revision by G. Vermes, F. Millar, and M. Black of E. Schürer, *History of the Jewish People in the Age of Jesus Christ (175 B.C.-A.D. 135)* 2 vols. (Edinburgh, 1973-).

the critics of the Empire make too much of these minor blemishes; in a famous judgment Gibbon justly observed,

> If a man were called to fix the period in the history of the world during which the condition of the human race was most happy and prosperous, he would, without hesitation, name that which elapsed from the death of Domitian to the accession of Commodus.[15]

One may still raise the question, Why the prosperity? The restoration of internal order by August and a reasonably efficient government, even in the hands of amateurs, strengthened local autonomy and enterprise;[16] in contrast to current orthodoxy it is clear that leading elements in Puteoli, in Aquileia and other cities either directly engaged in commerce and industry or supported slaves and freedmen as their agents.[17] Increase in production in the end rested, however, on a growing population, but not on greater productivity.

Problems in this regard became more severe as emperor succeeded emperor. The costs of government went up steadily, as in a necessary increase in the size of the army and more numerous equestrian procuratorships.[18] For reasons still obscure the population of the Empire evidently began to turn down in the second century, long before the era of troubles, though this shift can only be assessed impressionistically, not statistically. The "more honorable" upper classes became distinct in law from the "more humble" and seem to have exploited more directly their privileged position;[19] Herodes Atticus, for example, hit, robbed, and even killed free men, secure in his friendship with governors and Marcus Aurelius. The frontiers became more permeable as barbarians were allowed to settle within the Empire, and civilized skills accompanied gold subsidies to the tribes without the pale.

In the third century the result was internal chaos, centrifugal splintering as parts of the Empire broke away, and severe external

---

[15]*Decline and Fall of the Roman Empire*, ed. J.B. Bury, 1 (London, 1909), pp. 85-86.

[16]The amateur aspect has been recently stressed by R.P. Saller, *Journal of Roman Studies*, 70 (1980), pp. 44-63, and by Brunt in several essays.

[17]J.H. D'Arms, *Commerce and Social Standing in Ancient Rome* (Cambridge, Mass., 1981); so too R. MacMullen, *Roman Social Relations 50 B.C. to A.D. 284* (New Haven, 1974), c. 4. J.J. Wilkes, *Dalmatia* (London, 1969), gives specific examples.

[18]H.G. Pflaum, *Les Procurateurs équestres sous le Haut-Empire romain* (Paris, 1950), p. 106, estimates salaries of this type of official quintupled by the time of Septimius Severus.

[19]P. Garnsey, *Social Status and Legal Privilege in the Roman Empire* (Oxford, 1970).

threats. Here we need not tarry long on the host of disasters; after Dio Cassius and the feeble Herodian our literary sources are reduced almost exclusively to the Historia Augusta, a dreary collection of imperial biographies which have received far more attention than they warrant — there appears to be a historical law that the more obscure and insignificant a topic the more scholarly energy will be expended on it. The coinage of the Greek cities in bronze almost stops;[20] that of the emperor's mints becomes thin and repetitious in themes, though the evidence of hoards in Gaul helps us to trace the course of barbarian raids. Epigraphic material also drops off amazingly. So the efforts of Alföldi, MacMullen, and others to penetrate the murk probably will never allow us to see developments clearly, but certainly we must allow for considerable local variations in disasters and reactions.[21] Britain, for example, was almost untouched by external threats, and its rural villa owners seem to have prospered in the third century.

When one leaves behind the third century, the skies grow more serene for several generations, though the respite was only temporary. For the Late Empire we are fortunate in having two detailed and judicious surveys of its political history;[22] the sources themselves are more varied and extensive than for any era since the last century of the Republic, and include works by some of the major figures of the period. In my 1960 essay I noted that the fourth century had begun "to gain some attention in its own right, rather than as simply an era of decline best left to medievalists,"[23] and in the succeeding twenty-five years a great deal of valuable work has intensified this interest.

We still lack a full-scale biography of Diocletian, but Constantine has been frequently treated, though too much in his relations to Christianity rather than as a reorganizer of the governmental

---

[20]T. Jones, *Proceedings of the American Philosophical Society*, 107 (1963), surveyed the mints of Asia Minor in a preliminary fashion; much remains to be done.

[21]A Alföldi, *Cambridge Ancient History*, 12 (1939), cc. 5-6; R. MacMullen, *Roman Government's Response to Crisis A.D. 235-337* (New Haven, 1976); M. Mazza, *Lotte sociali e restaurazione autoritaria nel 3. secolo d. C.*(Catania, 1970).

[22]E. Stein, *Geschichte des spätrömischen Reiches 284-476*, 1 (Vienna, 1928); A.H.M. Jones, *The Later Roman Empire 284-602*, 3 vols. (Oxford, 1964; reprint 1974). See on the social side P. Brown, *The World of Late Antiquity* (London, 1971).

[23]*Journal of Roman Studies*, 50 (1960), p. 157.

structure.[24] Here we come to an aspect of the history of the Empire which has not been noticed in earlier pages but can no longer be ignored. Even for the first two centuries after Christ Christian sources, from the letters of Paul on, afford light on social conditions and, as is now recognized, not just those of the lowest classes;[25] in the third century the volume of this literature expands greatly. Yet there is an unfortunate tendency for secular and religious historians to pursue different paths, parallel chronologically but topically sundered; only in the matter of persecutions, the causes and legal justifications of which are still much debated, do state and church touch intimately.[26]

In the fourth century such a separation is no longer possible. The state interfered in ecclesiastical organization and dogma from the council of Nicaea onwards; in return religious leaders such as Hosius, Eusebius, and many later firm-minded bishops spoke out their mind on actions of the emperors. What earlier citizen of the Empire would have ventured to attack an emperor as did Lucifer of Cagliari, abusing Constantius as "the filth of all the sewers," "founder of blasphemy," and so on?[27] When Ambrose firmly banned the emperor Theodosius from the church at Milan for his bloody massacre at Thessalonica until he made penance, the interweaving of church and state had become complete, and on even terms at least in the West. It thus remains a puzzle as to how far heresies such as Donatism and Pelagianism were purely religious in character or reflected social distress of the lower classes.

Yet the economic and political deterioration of the absolutist state reared by Diocletian and Constantine cannot be measured simply by a Christian yardstick. In two masterful essays Alföldi traced the consolidation of late imperial court ceremony and imperial dress in

---

[24]So recently T.D. Barnes, *Constantine and Eusebius* (Cambridge, Mass., 1981), and *The New Empire of Diocletian and Constantine* (Cambridge, Mass., 1982). S. Williams, *Diocletian and the Roman Recovery* (London, 1985), is a general survey.

[25]W.A. Meeks, *The First Urban Christians* (New Haven, 1983), sums up recent studies especially in c. 2. The works of Sir William Ramsay, though now aged, are not without value.

[26]In the abundant literature see G.E.M. de Ste Croix, *Past and Present*, 26 (1963), pp. 6-38; W.H.C. Frend, *Martyrdom and Persecution in the Early Church* (Oxford, 1965); T.D. Barnes, *Journal of Roman Studies*, 60 (1970), pp. 32-50, ending "It is in the minds of men, not in the demands of Roman law, that the roots of the persecution of the Christians in the Roman Empire are to be sought."

[27]*Corpus Scriptorum Ecclesiasticorum Latinorum* 14 (K. Setton, *Christian Attitude towards the Emperor in the Fourth Century* [New York, 1941], p. 97).

secular context; and there has been more thoughtful attention to the system of taxation, the place of the distressed *curiales*, and the virtual enslavement of the rural population, illuminated by the edicts of the *Theodosian Code*.[28] In reality, however, there was more mobility in the Late Empire than ever before; laws, however severe, increasingly became divorced from reality. The actual course of change has been traced intensively for several areas of the Empire; more remains to be done. The cities of the western provinces declined in strength across the third and fourth centuries, an important shift often noted but still not adequately explained; the degree to which urban life in the west went on after 476 is uncertain.[29]

Culturally the activity in every field in the temporary restoration of the Late Empire is impressive testimony to its revival for a time. Wealth was now concentrated more narrowly in the hands of emperors, aristocrats, and bishops; Trier, Milan, Rome, Constantinople, and other cities were embellished with palaces and basilicas. Although late Roman art was the subject long ago of one of the most significant contributions to the theory of art history, its qualities were much depreciated until the present generation, which has produced very useful monographs on sculpture, ivory, mosaics, and other art forms.[30] In literature the last great pagan historian, Ammianus Marcellinus, has recently been assessed as perhaps the most judicious chronicler of all imperial history;[31] Christian scholars produced a great mass of letters, sermons, and treatises, the greatest of which flowed from the ever vigorous pen of Augustine, who has received his due in works by Marrou and Brown. The latter, one of the most sensitive and thoughtful scholars of recent years, has explored the role of the saint and kindred topics in all their psychological and spiritual complexity.[32]

And so to the last stage of ancient history, which gave rise to the great work noted at the beginning of this chapter. The Decline and

[28]A. Alföldi, *Die monarchische Repräsentation im römischen Kaiserreich* (Darmstadt, 1977); A. Cerati, *Caractère annonaire et assiette de l'impôt foncier au Bas-Empire* (Paris, 1975).

[29]E. Ennen, *The Medieval Town* (New York, 1979), is uncertain; much more archeological investigation is called for.

[30]A. Riegl, *Spätrömische Kunstindustrie*, 2 vols. (Vienna, 1901-23); English transl. by R. Winkes and R.R. Holloway (but only, I think in part; Rome, 1985).

[31]E.A. Thompson, *The Historical Work of Ammianus Marcellinus* (Cambridge, 1947); M.L.W. Laistner, *The Greater Roman Historians* (Berkeley, 1947); G.A. Crump, *Ammianus Marcellinus as a Military Historian* (Wiesbaden, 1975).

[32]A. Murray, *Journal of Roman Studies*, 73 (1983), pp. 191-203, provides a useful overview of Brown's work.

Fall has continued to mesmerize scholars as well as the general public, a bizarre example of which will conclude our survey. Simply to list all the varied explanations of the end of the Roman Empire occupies a sizeable volume,[33] amusingly enough exactly the same range can be found in explanations of the Mayan collapse, the end of the Indus River civilization, or the destruction of the Mycenanean palaces.[34] Thus some scholars seek the root in factors outside human control; one of my favorites in this area is the discussion of soil exhaustion by two Oklahoma agronomists — here, as is often the case, the authors have a modern axe to grind.[35] Others find the causal factors within the human framework; conservative journals and politicians repeatedly adduce the evil effects of absolutism, state socialism and other evidence of economic and political deterioration in the Decline and Fall.[36] Simpler in concept is the school which attributes the collapse purely to external invasions; the Roman Empire was "murdered."[37]

Obviously it is as impossible that we should all agree on one line of explanation as that we should concur in assessing the character and motives of Alexander the Great; each of us has his preconceptions and point of view. Yet the parameters within which a serious discussion must be phrased have been better defined in recent work. The increasing separation of the late aristocratic circles from the state has been judiciously explored; after all the aristocracy survived the end of the Empire in the west and made its accommodation with the successor kingdoms. So too the actual course of the barbarian invasions has been carefully analyzed, and also the concomitant

[33]A. Demandt, *Der Fall Roms* (Munich, 1984), gives 210 factors; see also the thoughtful discussion by S. Mazzarino, *The End of the Ancient World* (London, 1966). W.A. Oldfather delivered an early set of Sather lectures, never published, on the causes; in my years at Illinois I was never able to ferret out his manuscript, if indeed there was one.

[34]R.E.W. Adams, in T. Patrick Culbert, ed., *The Classic Maya Collapse* (Santa Fe, 1973), pp. 489-91, sets out succinctly the range of explanations; for the end of the Indus River civilization see M. Wheeler, *Civilizations of the Indus Valley and Beyond* (New York, 1966), pp. 72-83.

[35]T. Dale and V.G. Carter, *Topsoil and Civilization* (Norman, 1955).

[36]See the vehement introduction by C. Pharr to *The Theodosian Code* (Princeton, 1952); from the proper database one could retrieve abundant citations of the Decline and Fall in the *Wall Street Journal* and elsewhere.

[37]A. Piganiol, *L'Empire chrétien* (Paris, 1947), p. 422.

decline of military strength of the Roman army in the fifth century.[38]

Certainly explanations in terms of one factor are to be distrusted, for either such causes — lead poisoning for example — can be shown to be constants or alternatively are merely attendant circumstances. One should work on a much broader canvas. I know only one serious work which embraces, and at that in a short study, both the rise and fall of Rome, written by Montesquieu over two centuries ago, but there is much to be said for the the concept that the Decline and Fall represents the end of a long chain of evolution, "consumed by that which it was nourish'd with" (to adapt Shakespeare slightly).

It is, nonetheless, still possible to advance totally new explanations. The well-known TV star, Joan Collins, has moaned about herpes, AIDS, and so on, and concludes, "A good reason for celibacy. It's like the Roman Empire. Wasn't everybody running around just covered in syphilis? And then it was destroyed by the volcano."[39] I cite this not from flippancy but to support the point which I made earlier, that of all secular events in the ancient world the Decline and Fall has sunk most deeply into our consciousness.

Not that it was altogether "a bad thing." A recent study, indeed, can see in the darkness of the fifth century "the lurid flames of burning cities and farmsteads . . . the human pain which accompanied and followed the fall of the western Roman Empire is beyond even the figures of astronomy to calculate;"[40] but this is meaningless rhetoric. The priest Salvian was closer to the mark when he bitterly observed, "In the districts taken over by the barbarians, there is one desire among all the Romans, that they should never again find it necessary to pass under Roman jurisdiction."[41] In a lengthy discussion of the massive intellectual shifts in the Roman Empire, which led to a new view of man and his world, I even concluded that "the decline of the Empire was necessary for further progress,"[42] a judgment to which I would still hold.

---

[38]J. Matthews, *Western Aristocracies and Imperial Court, A.D. 364-425* (Oxford, 1975); E.A. Thompson, *Romans and Barbarians* (Madison, 1982); J.M. O'Flynn, *Generalissimos of the Western Roman Empire* (Edmonton, 1983); A. Ferrill, *The Fall of the Roman Empire: The Military Explanation* (London, 1986).

[39]*Playboy*, April 1984, p. 66.

[40]S.I. Oost, *Galla Placidia* (Chicago, 1968), pp. 280-81.

[41]*On the Governance of God* 5. 8.

[42]*Civilization and the Caesars* (Ithaca, 1954), p. 381. Hegel is as useful a thinker for the historian as many of his German successors.

V

GENERAL

The preceding chapters have treated the major eras of Greek and Roman history; now we must shift to more general topics, first the use of sources and therafter several issues much debated nowadays.

Down into the nineteenth century historians perforce used almost exclusively literary sources. A few monuments stood above ground; there were some inscriptions and coins available, which had been discussed especially by antiquarians from the Renaissance onward. But it was difficult to be certain that one had the exact text of an inscription, and individual coins by themselves gave only limited information.

Boeckh began the process of careful edition of Greek inscriptions; after his initial *Corpus Inscriptionum Graecorum* a new publication, *Inscriptiones Graecae*, carried on, but without Boeckh's drive so that even today it remains sadly incomplete. Mommsen did much better on the Latin side, enlisting many able scholars to tackle the inscriptions of the Empire province by province. These days, unfortunately, new collections of Latin inscriptions tend to be published on the basis of modern political units rather than Roman provinces, so that one has to consult a wide variety of works of limited scope.[1] In the same era archeologists began to produce evidence hidden for two millennia underground, and continue to enlarge and deepen our knowledge. Truth to tell, it is not easy for the general historian to understand site plans and photographs of the foundations of walls, and we do not always get the guidance which might be expected from our kindred experts; archeologists are taught early to concentrate on the specific item rather than to generalize, and can be wrapped on the knuckles by their elders if they do so. To quote one review, greater value would have resulted in a work under discussion "from a more limited application of his interpretive devices to the material and region with which he was thoroughly familiar."[2] Nor do

[1]See, for example, the list of recent publications in J. Reynolds, *Journal of Roman Studies,* 66 (1976), p. 175. For students lacking Latin or Greek we are now getting collections of translated inscriptions, as C.W. Fornara, *Archaic Times to the End of the Peloponnesian War* (Baltimore, 1977); N. Lewis and M. Reinhold, *Roman Civilization,* 2 vols. (New York, 1951-55); and others.

[2]J.B. Griffin, *American Journal of Archaeology,* 63 (1959), p. 414; for an unhappy example of accidental generalization by archeologists see my essay in *Generalization in the Writing of History,* ed. L. Gottschalk (Chicago, 1963), p.16 = *Essays on Ancient History,* p. 28.

archeologists always criticize freely the faulty work of other excavators at least until they are dead; the historian must identify weaknesses for himself.

Useful publication of numismatic evidence is a much more recent advance. Early in the twentieth century Babelon and Head reduced Greek issues to reasonable order, but the voluminous coinage of the Roman Empire had to wait until the 1920's, when Mattingly began publication of the coins of the Early Empire in the British Museum, one of the most creative and valuable works of the past generation and fortunately continued on into the Late Empire by other scholars.[3] A number of Greek mints have also received careful attention,though once again the historian should be wary of taking numismatic publications as gospel; an egregious example of completely misleading analysis is the now superseded study of Athenian coinage by Seltman. Even so numismatic evidence is now the frontier of ancient studies; in previous pages I have deliberately stressed its value at many points, and without doubt its potential future utility is of major order. A word of warning: anyone tackling a series of coinage which has not already been systematized must prepare to dig in a great number of works on public and private collections as well as inspecting the coins themselves; the fruits, however, may well repay the effort.[4]

Almost all historians, still, much prefer written evidence; Momigliano sums up this position, "I assume that the literary tradition, however doubtful, must still be our guide . . . no necropolis, however rich, can ever replace the living tradition of a nation."[5] So he himself, for example, does not adduce the useful information from sculptured busts in surveying the rise of Greek biography from the fourth century B.C. onward. I must confess myself amazed; where we would be studying early Attica if we did not have the magnificent evidence of the Kerameikos cemetery?

In another respect reliance on literary sources can be dangerous; nowadays it seems so difficult to say anything new that students sometimes impress into service very dubious materials. I have already commented on Huxley's reconstruction of several events in

---

[3]*Coins of the Roman Empire in the British Museum* (London, 1926-); he also wrote a magnificent general work, *The Man in the Roman Street* (New York, 1961).

[4]Here, as may be surmised, I am thinking of the European trips and long hours with a magnifying glass required to assemble the material in my *Athenian Coinage 480-449 B.C.* (Oxford, 1971).

[5]*Journal of Roman Studies,* 53 (1963), p.98.

early Spartan history purely from Pausanias; Diodorus has been used without warrant to supplement our scanty information on the mid-fifth century B.C.;[6] for Alexander Curtius Rufus has been brought to bear often without justification. The most extreme example is a recent life of Themistocles which baldly admits that the ''letters of Themistocles'' are a fabrication by a sophist in the second century after Christ and goes on to use them as evidence. Grote would have been stupefied.

Where there are solid historical texts, they are without doubt primary, for they give a connected account; but even in these cases the historian must be prepared to enrich his tale by the information to be derived from numismatic, epigraphic, and archeological materials. ''If so much can be made of archaeology before the beginning of writing, why can only so little be made of it afterwards?'' is a valid question.[7]

The following pages will be devoted to brief treatments of a variety of topics which extend across the whole of ancient history. A large number of subjects are available; I have chosen the role of women, slavery, imperialism, the use of Marxist doctrines, economic history, and the value of comparative evidence partly to illustrate areas which currently are very popular. Taken individually, these discussions may appear disjointed; but as a whole they are intended to support my final remarks on the gravest problem facing all ancient historians today.

We have recently made the interesting discovery that a very large part of ancient humanity was female. Exploitation of this discovery has sometimes been conducted by feminine scholars who are reacting against the difficulties faced by their twentieth-century peers, and so studies do not always have the witty, imaginative tone of the protest by Morgan against the exaggerated role of men as great hunters in prehistoric society.[8] It is, however, possible to write more objectively and illuminate, for example, the economic position of women in Greek society with unexpected results,[9] nor should one overlook the

---

[6]Meiggs, *Athenian Empire,* pp. 447-58, has a cautionary appendix on the use and misuse of Diodurus.

[7]G. Buccelloti, *American Historical Review,* 89 (1984), p. 1055.

[8]Elaine Morgan, *The Descent of Woman* (London, 1972).

[9]D.M. Schaps, *Economic Rights of Women in Ancient Greece* (Edinburgh, 1979). See also J.P. Gould, *Journal of Hellenic Studies,* 100 (1980), pp. 38-59; E. Burck, *Die Frau in der griechisch-römischen Antik* (Munster, 1969); and most recently S.B. Pomeroy, *Women in Hellenistic Egypt* (New York, 1984).

thoughtful, if discursive remarks of Ste Croix on women as a definitely productive part of society.[10]

One may hope that Gomme and Andrewes have dispelled the picture of Athenian wives as immured in harem life, suggested by the pompous Xenophon and others.[11] It is, however, unfortunately true that the only ancient author to evaluate womankind fairly was Musonius Rufus. A number of aspects in this area seem likely to repay investigation: the remarkable position of women in Spartan society certainly deserves more than brief notice;[12] the reasons for which Roman historians explained turning points in the Early Republic as the result of outraged women merit attention, and the role of aristocratic women in the Late Republic was often significant — consider the pressure Cicero's wife placed on him in the Bona Dea scandal. The psychological and religious forces which led late Roman aristocrats like Melania the Younger and Macrina to turn away from the world also demand fuller exploration.[13]

The enslavement of one human being to the will of another by force is a degradation of humanity, rightly deplored by Christians, agnostic humanists, and Marxists alike. The amount of money and effort that has gone into the factual study of slavery in many aspects in recent years is staggering — whereas aristocracies, which did set the intellectual tone of ancient culture, are ignored as a sacrifice to our contempt of elitism.[14] Yet if an institution such as slavery appears all over the ancient world from China to Greece and Rome there must have been powerful forces leading to its presence; and it is the duty of the historian, while hostile intellectually, to explore those reasons.

[10]G.E.M. de Ste Croix, *The Class Struggle in the Ancient Greek World* (Ithaca, 1981), pp. 98ff.

[11]Cf. also my essay on flute girls, *Parola del Passato,* 33 (1979), pp. 401-10, the most highly trained and profitable profession open to women in classical Athens. At least five works on Athenian courtesans existed in antiquity, and there were sex manuals as well as straightforward pornography (J. Griffin, *Journal of Roman Studies,* 67 [1977], p. 20).

[12]J. Redfield, *Classical Journal,* 73 (1977-8). pp. 146-61, does not exhaust the subject, which is treated to some extent in Schaps and in general histories of Sparta.

[13]See A. Momigliano, "The Life of St. Macrina by Gregory of Nyssa,"*The Craft of the Ancient Historian,*pp. 443-58.

[14]For a selection of bibliography of slavery, which is now vast, see M.I. Finley, *Ancient Slavery and Modern Ideology* (London, 1980). Russian views may be found in works by E.M. Staerman on the Republic (Wiesbaden, 1969), and Empire (1964); and the recent *Slavery in Babylonia* by M.A. Dandamaev (DeKalb, 1984), who concludes "slavery never reached in Babylonia such a degree of development that one can speak of slave labor as having the leading role in the economy."

Moreover, one should always keep in mind the fact that even so-called "free men" were often in a position of total subjection, exploited so that a very small minority might live well.[15] In a technologically simple world that is the important fact: the many had to work to support the luxury and pomp of the few.

Very distressing in modern studies of ancient slavery is the tendency to take it as the root cause of many ills or deficiencies. Thus the decline of Hellenistic science is attributed to slavery, whereas inadequate metal technology and a limited range of measuring instruments were probably more significant factors;[16] again the Decline and Fall have been explained as a consequence of slavery, "a cancer in the flesh of society which grew with society itself," a statement typical of the rhetoric often involved in discussions of slavery, and erroneous to boot — legal bondage was markedly declining in the Late Empire.[17] Years ago I made the grave error of expostulating against this simplicistic outlook and received as a reward attacks from both an American historian and a Russian scholar.[18] Only once, as far as I know, has the essay been praised; usually it has been ignored. More than anywhere else in ancient history there is an orthodoxy here which is not to be questioned. The closest parallel, also involving emotional reactions, is the general revulsion at Roman gladiatorial games in which even in the intermission "men were strangled lest people be bored." Without admiring bloodshed, nonetheless, the recruitment, training, and organization of the gladiatorial profession deserves investigation as a reflection of the skill and efficiency of Roman administrative structure, visible also in the general provision of water and food supplies even to moderate-sized cities; one might remember that the largest building in most Western centers was the amphitheater.[19]

Imperialism is another phenomenon much discussed these days,

---

[15]P. Garnsey, ed., *Non-Slave Labour in the Greco-Roman World* (Cambridge, 1980). A careful scholar such as Ste Croix always qualifies his condemnation of slavery by adding that free men were also exploited.

[16]B. Farrington, *Greek Science* (London, 1953); F. Kiechle, *Sklavenarbeit und technischer Fortschritt im römischen Reich* (Wiesbaden, 1969).

[17]F.W. Walbank, *The Awful Revolution* (Toronto, 1979), p. 61.

[18]*Journal of Economic History,* 18 (1958), pp. 17-32 = *Essays on Ancient History,* pp. 43-58; C. Degler, in the same journal, 19 (1959), pp. 271-77; J.A. Lencman, *Die Sklaverei im mykenischen und homerischen Griechenland* (Weisbaden, 1966).

[19]G. Ville, *La gladiature in Occident des origines à la mort de Domitien* (Paris, 1981), bears only incidentally on the aspect noted in my text. The quotation is from Seneca, *Epistles* 7. 5; not all Romans were fond of games.

and always unfavorably.[20] Judgments on ancient empires, however, have not been so uniformly hostile. Ever since the ancient Hebrew exultation over the fall of Nineveh, the Assyrian empire has not had a good press, remarkable though its achievement was in uniting the Near East politically. Its bloodthirsty joy in victory, celebrated both in great reliefs and in royal inscriptions in honor of Assur, does not encourage admiration. The Persian empire, on the other hand, has usually been treated neutrally or favorably, even though Greek opinion considered it a despotism in which all but one man were slaves. Again the Athenian empire, as noted in my first chapter, escapes condemnation; the most severe attacks have been reserved for the Roman empire, even though it was not in any legal sense an empire after Caracalla's gift of citizenship in A.D. 212.

One weakness in the treatment of imperialism, both modern and ancient, has been the emphasis since Hobson and Lenin on its economic causation. The French occupation of Tunisia, for example, can scarcely be explained in these terms, and one must remember the dedicated Christian missionaries, as significant in spreading political occupation as were traders and entrepreneurs; Hobson, amusingly enough, built his thesis almost entirely on the career of Cecil Rhodes, a very untypical example of English expansion.[21] Harris, let me recall, explored Roman imperialism largely in terms of the social aspirations of aristocrats; in this approach he is well supported by Schumpeter, who discussed the rise of the Persian empire as a good illustration of the ambitions of upper classes throughout history.[22]

With all the good will in the world I cannot detect in major works by Ste Croix and de Martino that their Marxist approach is the source of their strength, and in the case of lesser studies the distortion of historical reality to support a predetermined point of view becomes a glaring defect.[23] More generally Marxist doctrine in the strict sense, as expounded in *Das Kapital* — arising, let us remember, from

---

[20]P.D.A. Garnsey and C.R. Whittaker, edd., *Imperialism in the Ancient World* (Cambridge, 1978).

[21]J. Flint, *Cecil Rhodes* (Boston, 1974), pp. 228-29.

[22]*Imperialism and Social Classes* (New York, 1955), pp.3-98.

[23]Ste Croix, *Class Struggle*, F. de Martino, *Storia della costituzione romana*, 6 vols. (new ed., Florence, 1975), and *Storia economica di Roma antica*, 2 vols. (Florence, 1979). Lesser works include Walbank, *The Awful Revolution;* E.M. and N. Wood, *Class Ideology in Ancient Political Theory* (Oxford, 1978), which has a "trivialmarxischen" approach as it is put by H. G. Gehrke, *Gnomon*, 52 (1980), p. 179; and worst of all, M.O. Wason, *Class Struggles in Ancient Greece* (London, 1947). I regret that I have not seen L. Capogrossi, ed., *Analisi marxiste e società antiche* (Rome, 1978).

early nineteenth-century English capitalisn — does not appear very relevant to any era of ancient history, which lacked capitalist entrepreneurs and a true wage-earning class. Finley, as others, would prefer to assess ancient "class" divisions in terms of status, "an admirably vague word," so vague indeed that I do not see its use markedly aids our analysis of ancient social structure.[24] Again, both Greek and Latin historians were well aware of the evil effects of "class struggle";[25] depreciation of slavery is not exclusively a Marxist preserve; and as just noted the Marxist concept that imperialism must arise out of economic causes is not without question.

Nonetheless those of us who live in the capitalistic West would do well to keep our eye especially on Russian colleagues, who do operate in a different conceptual framework and since World War II have been producing valuable work.[26] If I were to give useful advice to a budding historian it would be to learn Russian as well as all the other ancient and modern languages he must possess; only in part can we tap Russian books and articles in *Vestnik Drevnei Istorii* through summaries or translations especially into German. It has always interested me in this regard that Russian scholars themselves no longer always make obeisance to Marx and Lenin in their opening lines whereas students in the Eastern satellites such as Oliva or Welskopf still find this usually obligatory. I shall never forget a lunch with a Belgian, Dutchman, and Pole during which it became *my* responsibility to defend a brilliant paper by Diakonoff of Leningrad against their attacks.

Study of economic developments we now think vital in historical analysis of modern societies, but it becomes very difficult for various reasons when we turn to the ancient world. One basic problem, the almost total lack of statistics, was stressed by Jones in an inaugural lecture.[27] Only at a few points do commensurate data in some

[24]M.I. Finley, *The Ancient Economy* (Berkeley, 1973), p. 51. Meeks, *The First Urban Christians*, pp.53-55, is a specific illustration of the complexities involved in measuring status and its many dimensions. Nowadays we may feel more comfortable, even so, with a general social term; the governing circles of early modern Europe might have not been so reluctant to think in terms of class.

[25]J.P. Vernant, *Eirene*, 4 (1965), pp. 5-19; S. Lauffer, *Historische Zeitschrift*, 175 (1958), pp. 497-514.

[26]A recent survey is in H. Heinen, ed., *Die Geschichte des Altertums im Spiegel der sowjetischen Forschung* (Darmstadt, 1980); M. Raskolnikoff, *La recherche soviétique et l'histoire économique et sociale du monde hellénistique et romain* (Paris, 1975).

[27]A.H.M. Jones, *Ancient Economic History* (London, 1948).

quantity lie at our disposal, as in the Delos temple records or the manumission inscriptions of Delphi, skillfully explored by Hopkins;[28] the effort on the other hand by Duncan-Jones to present quantitative data puts together disjoined material.[29] Years ago at an international meeting I received fascinating information that at Munich there was a great project to put all known ancient wages and prices on punch cards. I could only blink at the waste of effort, for both measures of quantity and values of coinage varied uncontrollably even in the limited area of Ptolemaic Egypt.

So we can look at ancient economic developments only in an impressionistic fashion, but to make matters worse we usually put on spectacles born of modern economic theory. At several points in preceding pages I have suggested my disagreement with this procedure and shall not go further here than to repeat that it is unwarranted to assume ancient upper classes had absolutely no interest in economic matters.[30]

Of late years there has been an increased willingness to make use of the comparative method, both factually and on the level of theoretical construct, though scholars such as Millar deliberately reject this approach, and many of us in making gingerly use of the social sciences resemble the African chieftan wittily described by Brown, who commented on a neighboring tribe: "They are our enemies. We marry them."[31] Culturally comparisons between ancient and modern times have little to recommend them. The argument that modern inhabitants of Tuscany have inherited artistic and other attitudes from the Etruscans, though a theory popular since the Renaissance, is without true foundations; again, Greek peasants of the twentieth century have had so long a stretch of Turkish rule and Orthodox faith that it is dangerous to draw parallels with the beliefs of men in the age of Hesiod.[32] If one, however, goes back before the Industrial Revolution and searches out information on

[28]Hopkins, *Conquerors and Slaves*, c. 3.

[29]R. Duncan-Jones, *The Economy of the Roman Empire* (Cambridge, 1974).

[30]A.E. Samuel, *From Athens to Alexandria* (Louvain, 1983), even detects in the fourth century B.C. a conscious economic theory, though not in terms of growth, a meaningless idea in a static world technologically appraised. The upper-class attitude still in Trollope's day forced a banker (*John Caldigate*, I, c.13) to approach his search for money "in a gradual, industrious manner, and in accordance with recognized forms."

[31]*Emperor in the Roman World*, p. xi; P. Brown, *Religion and Society in the Age of St. Augustine* (London, 1972), p. 119.

[32]P. Walcot, *Greek Peasants Ancient and Modern* (Manchester, 1971).

crop yields, one can establish a useful parameter of what ancient productivity of those peasants might have been.

Demographic principles and tables can also serve as a corrective to Kitto's idea that Greeks had long lives or to Boak's ill-founded remarks about manpower shortage in the Late Empire. Even today, however, so good a scholar as Snodgrass can postulate a 4% yearly increase in the population of eighth-century Attica, which is outside the bounds of the possible.[33] Hopkins has shown repeatedly how useful demographic information can be in constructing "models" of what might actually have occured in antiquity, and also illustrates in various works the proper application of sociological principles.[34] In particular he draws far less on Weber, Durkheim, and other theorists than do some colleagues. Even a pragmatic historian, true, must agree that we need to have theoretical concepts to marshal our ancient evidence into any useful order; but those concepts should not dominate in our reconstructions of "wie es eigentlich gewesen." (For the utility and dangers in turning to anthropology see my remarks in the first chapter.)

As I look back over the pages of this work I realize again that the solid work of many scholars has slipped through the meshes of my analyses; to give only one example of many, the studies by Casson on ships, seafaring, travel, and other topics are works of major utility, but none of them have been cited — this is, to repeat once more, not a bibliographical essay.

Some years ago Finley wrote despondently about the current state of investigations in ancient history.[35] One does not now see a George Grote or Theodor Mommsen; at least in the United States and Canada there are no powerful masters, who create schools of devoted followers — the students of Ferguson, Frank, Laistner, and others have followed their own paths.[36] Optimism still has its justification: the average dissertation accepted these days is markedly superior to one fifty years ago in the breadth and solidity of its research; so too

---

[33]My *Economic and Social Growth of Early Greece*, pp. 40-46; M.H. Hansen, *American Journal of Ancient History*, 7 (1982), pp. 174-75.

[34]But see the critiques by B.D. Shaw, *Helios*, n.s. 9 (1982), pp. 17-57, and *Classical Views*, 28 (1984), pp. 453-79.

[35]*Daedalus* 1977, pp. 129-42.

[36]M.A. Levi, *Journal of World History*, 12 (1970), pp. 435-51, is harsh on the failure even of immigrant scholars to create schools in the United States, but also criticizes antiquarian tendencies in English works in the manner of H. Last. Despite Syme's originality not one student has "really known how to assimilate his ideas."

the average monograph by the average scholar is much better reasoned than its parallel half a century ago. Certainly we cannot complain about the quantity of studies on aspects of ancient history, which steadily grows in bulk.[37] I am not sure, however, that our ability to command a general audience by presenting purely factual studies has risen; men such as Boissier no longer write for general journals, and in truth the literary style of our work has sunk abysmally, especially in England.[38] ''In America they haven't used [English] for years.''

Finally: the most critical problem affecting a great deal of work in ancient history in all eras. I have often noted how current interests and attitudes both motivate and distort our exploration of the past; if I am not mistaken this threat has become more apparent of late. Wilamowitz-Moellendorf made the famous remark that if we wish to revivify life which has passed away we must give our heart's blood to its spirits. Less often quoted are his next lines. ''We give it to them gladly; but if they abide our question, something from us has entered into them, something alien, that must be cast out, cast out in the name of truth!''[39] Most of us have decided to explore the varied nature of mankind by seeking it in its ancient setting, a marvelous window indeed; but even if we cannot totally divorce our minds from the world in which we live let us admire the Romans and Greeks for themselves:

> A changeable creature, such is man
> a shadow in a dream.
> Yet when god-given splendor visits him
> a bright radiance plays over him,
> and how sweet is life![40]

---

[37]Shaw, *Helios,* n.s. 9 (1982), p.52, counts in *L'Année philologique* for 1977-78 about 2000-2200 books and articles, an increase of 50% during a decade.

[38]*Greek Historical Writing* (Oxford, 1908), p. 25.

[39]P. Green is an exception, as in *Essays in Antiquity* (Cleveland, 1960), but he has now turned to a massive, forthcoming study on the Hellenistic age.

[40]Pindar, *Pythian* 8 (tr. Kitto).

GENERAL BIBLIOGRAPHY

There is no need here to present a bibliography of bibliographies; every textbook on ancient history will lead one into the sources and modern studies on any subject. A serious student of the ancient world should have, despite the expense, *Oxford Classical Dictionary* (2d ed.; Oxford, 1970), and *Der kleine Pauly* (Munich, 1954-75).

Two complementary works which might not immediately come to mind do deserve note. M. Hammond, *The City in the Ancient World* (Cambridge, Mass., 1972), has a remarkably complete survey of political and related literature (pp. 388-549). J.L. Tobey, *The History of Ideas: A Bibliographical Introduction,* 1 (Santa Barbara, 1975), covers intellectual aspects. Although flawed by mistakes and omissions (see the unreasonably contemptuous review in *Gnomon,* 50 [1978], pp. 231-35), Tobey has generally good judgment in his evaluations and treats a wealth of subjects.

Chester G. Starr was born in Missouri in 1914. He received his B.A. with Distinction from the University of Missouri in 1934, his M.A. from the same university in 1935, his Ph.D. from Cornell in 1938. His doctoral dissertation on the Roman imperial navy is still in print. From 1940 to 1970 he taught at the University of Illinois (minus four years in World War II, in which he became a lieutenant colonel in command of the Historical Section Fifth Army). From 1970 to 1985 he was at the University of Michigan, where he was awarded the Bentley professorship, Distinguished Faculty award, and Distinguished Faculty lectureship. He received an honorary degree from his alma mater in 1981, is a fellow of the American Academy of Arts and Sciences, and has held two Guggenheim fellowships.

His initial attention was directed to the Roman Empire, but after publishing *Civilization and the Caesars* (1954) he turned back to the formative era of classical civilization, which produced *The Origins of Greek Civilization* (1961) and a variety of other studies. To date he has published 21 books, a number of articles (which were collected by his students Arther Ferrill and Thomas Kelly in *Essays on Ancient History* [1979]), and 150-odd reviews. The Association of Ancient Historians, of which he was founding president, has issued in his honor *The Craft of the Ancient Historian*. The introductory essay in this volume, by E. Badian, is a thoughtful assessment of his work; another survey, by by A. La Penna of Florence, may be found in the Italian translation of the second edition of his *History of the Ancient World*.

70

P 7 n.24 Check